Creativity, Art, and the Young Child

Creativity, Art, and the Young Child

W. Lambert Brittain

CORNELL UNIVERSITY

Macmillan Publishing Co., Inc.
NEW YORK

Collier Macmillan Publishers
LONDON

Macmillan Publishing Co., Inc.
866 Third Avenue, New York, New York 10022

Collier Macmillan Canada, Ltd.

Library of Congress Cataloging in Publication Data

Brittain, W   Lambert.
   Creativity, art, and the young child.

   Bibliography: p.
   Includes index.
   1. Creative activities and seat work.
I. Title.
LB1537.B73   372.5   78-3635

Printing: *6 7 8*   *Year:*   *4 5*

ISBN   0-02-314990-6

Preface

I have strayed a little from my original intentions. Originally this book was conceived as putting together in one place the results of several studies done at Cornell University on the art of young children; it is an outgrowth of five years of research and experimentation. Support for the research came primarily from the National Laboratory on Early Childhood Education and through grants from the College of Human Ecology at Cornell. These studies have been reported in various ways, some as master's and doctoral theses and some in professional journals. However, in assembling these and seeing the relationship between the studies, it was necessary to refer at times to work done at places other than Cornell. Consequently, pertinent research from other resources has been incorporated so as to form a broad base for a better understanding of creativity and children's art.

v

The audience for this volume is primarily the teacher of young children. Every nursery school and kindergarten utilizes a large range of art activities. Many of these activities bear little relationship to the developing child. One of the purposes of this book is to focus upon the importance of creative activities in the development of cognitive competency. Past studies have paid little attention to the development of art forms by children up to the age of six. However, there is a clear developmental progression, and this book pursues the reasons for these changes in depth.

A good deal of emphasis is on the potential for creative behavior as a natural means of a child's organizing and utilizing environmental stimuli. Therefore a section of the book provides the teacher of young children with specific suggestions for methods for teaching creative activities in a meaningful way.

The book follows what seems like a natural progression. First are included observations of children engaged in art activities and some of their comments and reactions to the teaching environment. This is followed by a chapter which documents the stages of development in art and one which explains a little of the causes for these changes. The next section deals with the copying and discrimination ability of young children, since this is an important aspect of most nursery school programs; the experimentation that has gone on at Cornell raises some serious questions about the importance of these activities. This is followed by a chapter which looks at the use of materials and presents the results of studies which dispute customary practices. Next comes a chapter which deals with interpreting children's drawings, not just from a psychoanalytic viewpoint, but from intellectual and social perspectives as well. This is followed by a chapter which deals in detail with the role of the teacher. The next two chapters deal first with problems of aesthetics and perception and then with cognitive growth and its relationship to creative activities. The last chapter makes recommendations for a program which utilizes art and creative activities for stimulating intellectual and creative development. Here the book provides the teacher with do's and don'ts which are based on the information derived from our first-hand experience with children.

The many studies which form the basis for this work are in themselves interesting, and I may have done the authors an injustice by summarizing their findings. For those studies done elsewhere, which I have admittedly only referred to in passing, the bibliography carries the source for the reader who would like to pursue a question in more detail. The importance I see is not in the individual studies, but in the impact of the total as it demonstrates the importance of art for young children. Taken as a whole, I was impressed with the message that came across clearly. The creative arts are a rich source for learning that are largely ignored in school settings.

W. Lambert Brittain
Department of Human Development
    and Family Studies
Cornell University
Ithaca, New York

Acknowledgments

The original work on young children's art was begun several years ago with a research grant from the College of Human Ecology. However, the main support was from the Cornell Research Program in Early Childhood Education, a component of the National Laboratory on Early Childhood Education funded through the Office of Education, U.S. Department of Health, Education and Welfare. These funds helped support several graduate students and gave the impetus for our work in this area. Although graduate theses are listed in the bibliography, the discussions and advice of these knowledgeable people must be recognized. This includes Elizabeth Clarke, Pamela Collett, Beth Goertz, Harlan Holladay, Jane Hooper, Eric Mauer, Elizabeth Pawlikowski, Anna Sibley, Helen Stein, and Alice Trisdorfer. I was fortunate in having a great deal of help in observing children's behavior while they were involved in art activities. Help may not be the right word, for in some cases the direction of the work was altered because of the personal involvement of these people. This includes Yu-Chin Chien, Loren Davidson, Deborah Dowling, Joan Fox, Joan Green, Rachel Silverstein, Janet Shapiro, and Melissa Zeriakus. In addition several of the above people played the role of a teacher in the nursery school, as did Carol Ast, Anne Liebermann, and Janet Schmidt, when we tried some experimental programs. I am also grateful for help in obtaining the illustrations to Jane Hooper, Nancy Colletta, Judy Richland, Beth Wensch, and to Mme. Lapouge of the Ecole Maternelle, Souillac, Lot, France, for sharing the drawings and newspaper made by the children at her school.

Special mention must be made of the philosophic discussions with Armando Brissoni of Florence, Italy, while he was at Cornell. His thoughts were particularly helpful in putting together Chapter 9. A lot of the details and accuracy of references were checked with the help of Pat Semanek, and special mention should be made of Jane Hooper's careful reading of the manuscript. But most appreciated was the cooperation of the many nursery school teachers, particularly of the Cornell Nursery School, and of the many kindergarten teachers who allowed us to clutter up their rooms. Without the children there would have been no study, and I am deeply indebted for their patience in teaching us adults what art can mean for young children.

W. L. B.

Contents

1

Observations of Young Children

In the Nursery School

What art activities do young children engage in? What kind of products do they make? Does any learning take place during these activities? With the convenience of the Cornell Nursery School at hand, we began our investigations into the meaning and importance of art for preschool children. Our first contacts were informal, enabling us to establish rapport with the children and to get a better understanding of the task before us. Then we developed a more serious study, or rather a series of studies, based upon our initial observations.

It was a pleasant task to observe these nursery school children. Art in some form seemed to involve them for at least a part of every day. Several things

1

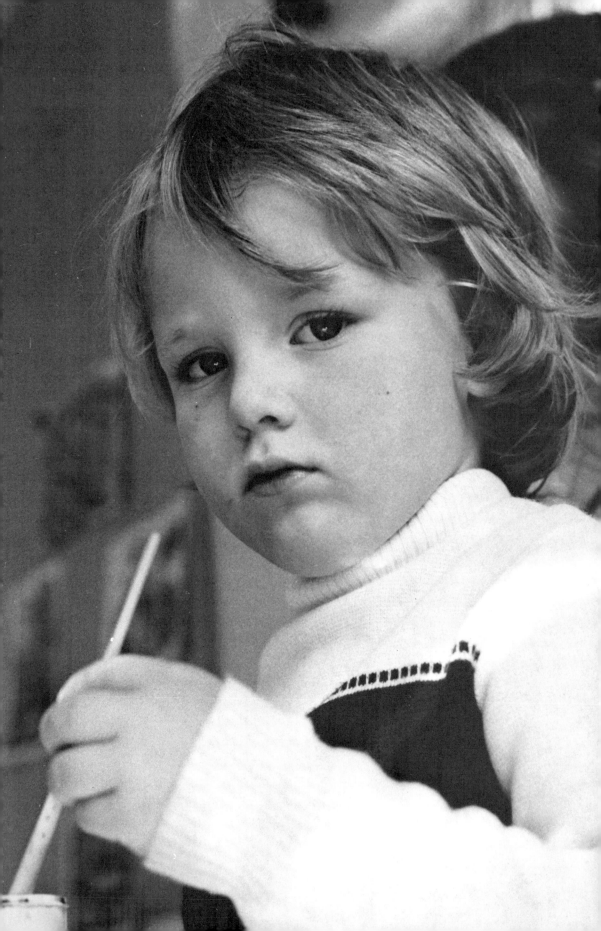

impressed us. The children were open about their art activities; there seemed to be no attempt to hide what they were doing, to conceal true feelings, or to perform for adults. This spontaneity made some of our work easier, but also somewhat more difficult when the children turned to us for help in buttoning up smocks or as respondents for conversation. This involvement became a problem when we were trying to determine interest level in various activities or trying to record comments between children, and found ourselves suddenly thrust into service as a holder for a very full paintbrush.

Observations were made intermittently over a period of five years by a number of different people. Some of the art activities were videotaped, but even this method did not seem to disturb the children's activities after their initial curiosity wore off. Not all of the data are presented here, but we have included enough of the background to give the reader an understanding of the basis for the inferences and tentative conclusions of our research.

The nursery school has changed its physical arrangement from year to year, but there are usually two easels for painting, small tables for drawing or science activities, open spaces, shelves with blocks and toys, bathroom facilities, books, puzzles, and a changing display of seasonal or educational material. The groups have varied somewhat in size and age, with 17 to 20 children, from just under three to just over five years of age, meeting in the morning and a somewhat comparable group in the afternoon. The children were primarily from middle-class homes, and a few disadvantaged children were bussed in; occasionally physically handicapped children would be in one of the groups.

Art plays a large role in most nursery schools, larger than in any other segment of the educational system. The Cornell Nursery School is no exception. Although the daily routine varies somewhat depending on the teacher, weather, or special events, there is usually an hour a day given over to individual or group art. This is often the first thing in the morning, with children joining small groups at the tables for some sort of creative activity or else having a turn at the easel to paint with big brushes on large sheets of

1. Art is a natural means of expression for nursery school children. They are not self-conscious about their work and often enjoy sharing their thoughts with adults.

paper. These activities continue with ups and downs in interest, as children change tables and are encouraged to participate in one or more of the current projects.

Although the center of our observation was the Cornell Nursery School, many observations were also made in a variety of other preschool programs: large schools supported by public funds, Head Start programs designed for disadvantaged children, small independently-run programs three mornings a week, and both rural and urban kindergarten classrooms. Rarely did the schools hesitate to accept observers. Looking at children involved in drawing or painting seemed not at all threatening to anyone, so we were pleased to be able to do our research in the guise of innocent, interested bystanders.

Children Painting at the Easel

Clean paper was placed on the easel. The paints were in salvaged juice cans in a row on the easel trough. At one observing session, a nursery school boy dipped his brush into the can of red paint at the left end of the easel tray, painted a single bold red stroke on the paper directly above the can, and returned the brush to the paint. Then he picked up the brush from the can of yellow paint, next to the red, painted a single bold yellow stroke beside the red one, and returned the brush to its can. He continued in this way, with green, blue, and black paints as he worked his way from left to right, using each paint in turn. Apparently satisfied that the job was done, he turned around and left the painting area and waited to be helped out of his smock. He had said nothing during this brief time.

A second boy, approaching painting with a smile on his face, said something that was interpreted as "I love mushy paint, I love to mush and dribble." He painted with vigor, paying little attention to which color he used but, instead, watched closely the strokes he made, almost in amazement that he could make such nice strokes. With his left hand he held the paper

2. *Sometimes children talk to themselves when painting, as if carrying on a conversation with their pictures.*

steady; as he filled the paper, the hand, too, soon became smeared with paint. When the page was filled, he commented, "See? Well, now I am finished."

At this time, a girl who had been waiting quietly took her position at the easel. She looked at each can of color and then picked up a clean brush; she dipped it into the yellow paint, painted several horizontal strokes, repeated her actions with the green paint, and frowned when the colors ran together. After contemplating her painting, she surrounded the whole

5

area with a frame of blue, whispered that she liked blue, and proceeded to take off her smock.

Two boys were next, and they seemed to be more interested in each other than in painting. They rapidly scribbled a color on the paper, looked more at each other than at their work, and proceeded to do one picture after another with giggles and comments about swishing paint faster than anybody. A few minutes later, a girl was busily painting a house which appeared as an outline, saying it was her house in California. Across the bottom of the paper was a green line which might have been intended as grass; however, the whole sheet was then colored red, right over everything, and the picture was apparently completed. In the meantime, one boy was mixing paint on the paper and painting what he called prehistoric animals, one round blob following another round blob. He talked to himself continuously, saying, "Dinosaurs eat each other." When the paper was filled with the gray blobs, he mumbled that this was all the dinosaurs that were living. He proceeded to the bathroom sink to wash his hands.

Our list of children could continue, but perhaps we should look more closely at these few we have been watching. There is more than enough evidence to say that each child is a unique individual, and that his approach to painting reflects this. Some children seem to be concerned primarily with the manipulative aspects of painting and enjoy the tactile sensation and the feel of paint. For others, it is the visual aspects that become more important; they are concerned with control over the form and with the selection of color. For still others, the symbol takes on meaning, whether it is a house or a dinosaur; the painting then becomes a representation of a particular event or series of events and shows some emotional involvement.

At the same time, there are similarities in the paintings that mark them as preschool art. There are no paintings of landscapes, no examples of carefully executed abstract designs, and no working from models. No child seemed annoyed at his inability to draw a particular object.

When one speaks of children drawing and painting, the usual image that comes to mind is of youngsters engaged in a pleasurable, happy activity, wearing

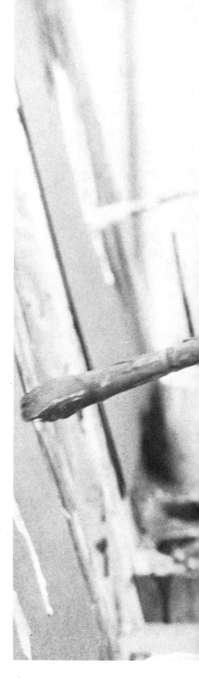

3. *Art is an important part of the daily routine in most preschools, and children treat this activity seriously.*

6

smocks, standing at easels which are just their size
and busily painting with bright colors. We expect the
paintings to be bold and colorful, filling the whole
paper with large forms. Because preschool children are
often considered to be spontaneous and free in drawing and painting, adults are apt to envy the child's
freshness and the uninhibited approach to painting. It
is no wonder that these drawings and paintings are

7

often displayed and that art activities play an important part in nursery schools and kindergartens.

Actually, however, that image of preschool painting is not totally accurate. Some children are reluctant
to paint, or the paint may be spilled, or painting
hands may be more enjoyable than painting paper, or

4. *Direct, bold appli-
cation of color gives a
feeling of freshness in
paintings by young
children.*

the paint may drip down the paper and frustrate the children. Reality is somewhere in between these two extremes of gleeful spontaneity and annoying frustration. Because of time limitations or lack of adult help, sometimes the use of paint, paper, and brushes is restricted in favor of other activities. The teacher is so busy preparing the paint, providing clean paper, washing the hands of those children who have finished painting, and hanging up completed paintings to dry, that there is often little opportunity to observe very much about the painting process itself.

Recording Children's Comments

The nursery school provided a good opportunity for us to collect comments children made as they painted. It was hoped that these comments would give some clue as to whether a child was trying to represent objects in his paintings. However, an observer might upset youngsters' painting habits by coming too close, so it was thought wise to find less obtrusive methods. A microphone connected to a tape recorder was placed by the nursery school easels, and it was turned on whenever a child decided to paint. Listening to these tapes later was a bore. Some interesting scratching noises of the brush were recorded, and an occasional humming sound from the child. The teacher's comments, such as, "Would you like another piece of paper?" when the painting was finished, were also recorded. But no new insights or descriptive revelations were obtained from what the child said. The adult did not seem to intrude upon the child's creative experience by being present; rather, the creative experience was nonverbal if there was no adult discussing the painting with the child or helping to arrange another sheet of paper.

The next step in this particular study was to have a friendly nursery school teacher talk to the children while they were drawing. Armed with a collection of colored felt-tipped pens, a genial teacher-type person asked individual children to draw at a somewhat isolated table. Obviously this case study approach would

5. *Felt-tipped pens are an excellent drawing tool for young children. The ink flows where it is wanted.*

have limited use for broad generalizations, but some rather interesting things appeared. Initially the purpose of the experiment was to have the teacher record a description of the drawing activity as it took place. It was hoped that describing the process quietly into a small tape recorder would provide observational notes which, compared with the finished products, might reveal some insights that were missed earlier when the tape recorder microphone was merely draped over the easels. As soon as the adult started making comments about the drawing procedure, such as, "John is drawing down the side of his paper and is now making a wiggly line along the bottom," the child interrupted to explain that the line was not a wiggly one, but indeed was water. "And with the red pen he is drawing a line up the right side of the page." "No!" said John, "that

6. *When a child draws, he does not begin with a definite plan, and his ideas remain flexible. The scribble is a record of his thinking.*

is a house and here is the button." It was from this give-and-take method, after most of the twenty children had completed one or more drawings, that inferences could be drawn.

A few of the children enjoyed talking as much as drawing. It became obvious that certain finished parts of the picture reminded a child of other things, so that the meaning of the drawing as it developed would change, and the completed parts would be incorporated into a new theme. When the picture was finished, both the drawing and the discussion often bore little resemblance to the theme that had seemed important at the beginning. For example, the wiggly line along the bottom of the paper, which had been water, could change into an angry dog running across the page. Adults and sometimes older children usually know what a picture is going to be before they begin; the picture usually isolates a particular theme or an event. However, these preschool children's drawings seemed to have no such preconceived image; rather, the picture was influenced by what was drawn, and the concept of what was coming next seemed very fluid. The completed drawing, therefore, turned out to be more a record of the youngster's thinking process than a concrete representation of a particular thought or image.

Some of the drawings did, in fact, resemble objects or people. But, even in those drawings that had no apparent visual reference, the scribble and lines did have meaning. The wavy lines, connoting water at one point, and in the next minute representing a dog running, were typical. The paper often became a map upon which the child drew the path of an object but not necessarily its visual representation. In some cases it seemed as if the pen or crayon figuratively became the object, as with the running dog, or rather that the drawn line imitated the action rather than depicting the object itself. Children seemed to put together in one place elements of their environment that they thought important, and the paper became a stage upon which these things moved.

Occasionally children would want to keep their drawings, but it was felt important that all of these drawings be filed for later study. The children were then told that they could have their drawings the next

7. *Painting boxes can be a challenging project. Here we see that the inside is just as important to paint as the outside.*

day. A few children did remember, but when shown three or four drawings they usually could not identify their own. Either they did not retain the image of what the finished picture was like, or else they had never really looked at their completed product. Probably it is the latter. One child wanted to have his paint-

13

ing back the next day and was told that of course he
could have it. However, when he came to claim it, he
spent a considerable length of time examining the
three or four paintings shown to him before finally
picking the right one. "Oh, I remembered that this is
mine because I mixed up all the paints." Apparently
the mixing process was what he recalled and not the
visual impression of the completed picture. Just as the
process of painting or drawing was what involved the
child, the completed product was remembered because
of the process itself. Drawing a line, mixing paint, and
filling in space was much more important than the
visual impression of the end result.

The relative unimportance of a completed appearance, inferred here, was further observed when children were painting cardboard boxes. The boxes were
large, about two feet long. Six or eight children found
this a worthwhile activity and continued at this task
for over half an hour. The boxes were not being
painted to represent houses, nor were they being used
as a surface upon which to experiment with color as
often seemed to be the case with easel painting. Instead, the boxes were considered boxes, and the challenge was to paint the sides. Alice had carefully
painted the top of one box with yellow paint. Although the surface was completely painted, a spot of
blue paint had been inadvertently dropped on one corner, so this had to be repainted several times until the
top was a smooth pure yellow. Once satisfied, she
took another box that same size and placed it right on
top of the yellow, completely covering the painted surface. Then she took masking tape and tried to tape
the upper box onto the lower. One of the adults
helped to steady the upper box until it was firmly
attached. Alice at this point was finished and ran off
to wash her hands. Although the appearance of the
yellow paint was important, it was not for display.
The work was done well, not for the eyes of others,
but for her own satisfaction. Perhaps there is an intuitive aesthetic awareness and integrity that is expressed
naturally at this age.

Drawings by children between the ages of three
and four are filled with symbols that have no visual
reference. These are sometimes referred to as haptic
representations. Some of the scribbles represent hurry-

up lines, jumping lines, or swinging lines; occasionally such tactile impressions as roughness and smoothness are represented. Even when the first visual representation appears, these additional lines are often included. It is not until about age five or six that these haptic or nonvisual lines become less frequent in children's drawings.

Videotaping the Drawing Process

An attempt was made to videotape the art processes of preschool children. The initial attempts were unsuccessful because of several technical problems. One-inch tapes were discarded in favor of the greater portability and versatility of half-inch tapes; used with a portable camera and battery-supplied current, these

8. *Learning how to use scissors is a struggle, but mastering the manipulation of the tool brings great satisfaction.*

made the task of following particular children much easier. The problem of sound reproduction was solved by supplying wireless microphones for individual children and picking up their voices through an FM receiver. This permitted easy monitoring of a conversation between a particular child and an adult.

Examination of the eight best twenty-minute tapes revealed that there are many things occurring in the creative process. For most children the use of art materials is a serious business. The gripping of the crayon, the holding of the brush, and the twisting of the clay are all done with a sense of purpose and urgency. We have no examples of a child's fooling around with art materials. One sequence shows a youngster trying to cut a piece of light cardboard with a pair of scissors. It is clear that this is a real struggle; although other things intervene, the task goes on for nearly fifteen minutes before completion. The satisfaction in completing the task is obvious, and no particular use was made of the pieces once they were cut. Apparently satisfaction comes from the sense of accomplishment and evolves from the process itself.

The role of the teacher was looked at closely. It seems that an adult can often be an intrusion as well as a help. For example, while one youngster was pasting a collage, the nursery school teacher, anticipating difficulty, assisted the child, who promptly stopped work on the collage and pushed it aside. In another sequence two girls were exchanging clay biscuits and pretending to eat them. The arrival of the teacher halted this bit of dramatic play, as if the children thought it was undesirable for an adult to see such play-acting. There are further assumptions that can be drawn from these tapes, but the testing of these hypotheses needs to be done systematically.

Use and Misuse of Activities

Nursery schools in the United States seem to follow a fairly consistent program, except for some minor variations when a particular syllabus is being followed or when emphasis is being given to certain aspects of development. Sometimes attention is given to language development or to the acquisition of certain types of information, such as color or form identification. The emphasis may be on eye–hand coordination, problem solving, or even on social skills (if learning to be quiet while someone else, usually the teacher, speaks, can be considered a social skill). These special objectives, sometimes referred to as the needs of a particular group of young children, often mean that the time for painting and drawing is diminished. Their rationale for limiting the time for creative activities is that this work is not as important for children as developing language skills or learning concepts. One program (Bereiter and Engelmann, 1966) went so far as to assume that there was no reason to include creative activities for children because these can supposedly be experienced outside the schoolroom. Often it is the poor or deprived children who are exposed to such strong-armed, noncreative programs. Yet when these children arrive in the public school, there is no evidence of any lasting improvement from the emphasis put on particular aspects of learning. This will be discussed further in Chapter 10.

9. A class of French preschool children visited their railway station. One child drew this picture to be included in the school newspaper with the story of the trip.

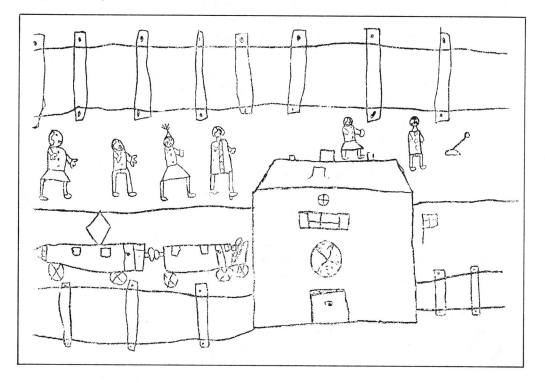

Probably the best known nursery school which restricts creative activities was initiated by Maria Montessori in Italy during the early 1900's. She worked with retarded children and developed a structured environment geared toward self-discipline and work. Although many materials and activities, such as tracing around geometric forms or certain sequential procedures, have been adopted in present day Montessori-type schools, some creative activities are often included. Montessori herself felt that scribbling was not an acceptable activity and that teaching children "how to draw" was what was important (Montessori, 1964).

The observations made as background for the present volume demonstrate the importance of children's art activities. Perhaps those who downgrade such experiences have never stopped to observe the seriousness with which children undertake drawing and painting. For example, one observation of a preschool in France showed that children viewed art as worthwhile work. There was a weekly newspaper produced by the children, consisting of drawings and some lettering, to tell of their activities of the past week. The older children ran the duplicating machine and distributed the paper to all classrooms in the school. Art activities included making sand bolsters for placing against the doors to stop drafts — a useful and customary piece of French home furnishing. Particularly for the younger children, there were ample supplies of small sheets of paper and colored drawing pens; the children worked hard drawing on these papers and then carefully filed them on shelves under their names.

Noncreative tasks are mistakenly called art by many nursery schools. Such activities include pasting macaroni into some sort of predetermined pattern, spilling colored sand onto wet glue, sticking toothpicks into styrofoam, dipping string into wet paint and wiggling it over paper, painting over doilies on a sheet of paper, threading together paper plates, and other projects that seem important to the nursery school teacher. However, except for the act of physical completion, these tasks do not truly involve the child. Observance of children engaged in these pseudo-art activities shows that they do not consider this work important to them; they talked less about the activity itself than when doing their own work, spent less time at these tasks, were easily distracted, and often had to be admonished to finish. The products of these directed lessons were similar to one another or to the model if one was used, except for those that were not finished or those that for some reason had been made incorrectly.

Preplanned art activities often have a good deal of the teacher's thinking imbedded in them, making it difficult to tell how much of a project is the child's. This became important when we saved children's art for later examination. Although we were tempted to save some of the more ridiculous examples dreamed up by enthusiastic teachers, such as cereal collages, paintings made with shaving cream from spray cans, or tongue depressors and ribbons pasted together, we found that these began to deteriorate rapidly; with some relief we abandoned that notion. Instead we concentrated upon drawings, paintings, and clay products, although the latter caused some storage problems. It was in the drawings that we found the greatest amount of information, because these could usually be counted upon to be the result of the child's own thinking.

Basic Assumptions

From our observations several conclusions can tentatively be made. A drawing or painting by a young child is not a record of past incidents, or a visual representation of the present such as one might expect from a photograph, nor is it a wish fulfillment for the future. Rather, a drawing or a painting by a preschool child is more an experience in itself, an experience with paints, a challenge which is manifest on the paper. This is not to say that children do not use symbols for objects in their paintings; they do. These symbols are not visual representations of objects; they are not attempts at a visual likeness. A house is merely a closed form; a person is a circle with dangling appendages. These forms or symbols stand for

an object in much the same way that words stand for objects for an adult.

Observations have also made it clear that drawing is thought of in the present tense. For a child, there was no plan to paint over a hand; rather, the hand was in the way and therefore it seemed logical to put paint on it at the time. There was no question of whether or not to paint over the house symbol with red; the red color was being put on and therefore the house was covered up too. In watching preschool children painting, one easily becomes involved in a conversation with the child, who eagerly shows his painting. One such child had drawn herself and her sister. Asked where the rest of the family was, she promptly replied, "At home." And when asked if her sister were at home too, the youngster pointed to the picture and replied that of course not, her sister was right here!

Sometimes it seems as if a preschool youngster draws what he can. One boy drew a circle with dots that appeared to be eyes, nose, and mouth and added two long lines below, which were probably legs. He called this his father. When the boy was encouraged to draw his father's car, his reply was simply that he could not draw cars. There is little in the way of apology at this age for lack of artistic skill. Possibly adults could learn something from this, since some of us tend to be apologetic about our own lack of artistic ability.

A youngster draws what he is interested in, and whatever is important to him at the time. The act of drawing seems to be an occasion in itself, and the child is engaged in the process rather than in producing a product recognizable to an adult. Sometimes he is eager to talk about what he is doing, and other times he does not want to talk about what he is doing, or painting seems just a way of passing time. Each child is unique in what he brings to the activity — his complex understandings, his purpose, his reactions in the process of self-expression.

10. *"Here is my sister." Children draw what is important to them; they do not attempt to draw a beautiful picture.*

2

Stages of Development in Art

Collecting Children's Art ─────────

Hundreds of drawings and paintings were saved during the several years of this study. Initially these were collected from whatever sources were available: from proud parents of two year olds, from nursery schools, and from kindergartens. From this collection we developed a feeling for the range and complexity of children's art and could then begin to collect drawings in a more systematic way.

We were forced to discard many products that we had gathered. Some fell apart as paste dried; the restrictions of space and the limited tolerance of the fire inspector meant disposing of a great deal more. However, most of the discarded art products had limited value for us. Many were so involved with some aspect

23

of teaching and were so preplanned that it was difficult to determine how much of the product actually
resulted from the child's thinking. Where various
shapes had been cut out by the teacher and the child's
task was merely to paste these onto a sheet of paper,
we saw little evidence to help us understand children
or their art. Also many "art" projects in both nursery
school and kindergarten almost seemed to be designed
to frustrate our efforts. When children painted with
cotton swabs, or dipped string into paint and dragged
it across the page, or used crumpled paper to apply
paint, or had plastic molds into which to push clay,
we found that these products showed no discernible
variation resulting from developmental level, no
uniqueness for individual children, and no evidence
of conscious ordering or control of the medium.

We did collect more than enough examples of
drawings, paintings, and clay pieces which reflected
both the child's intent and abilities. This collection
was later augmented with drawings made under controlled conditions, where all children used the same
standard materials — one size of paper and black
fiber-tipped pens — and all drew the same topic. We
wanted to compare differences in the drawing method
and in the way the topic was treated as children grew
older, without the confusion of different colors and
paper sizes. By dividing our collection into categories
according to the age of the child, we were able to
make some general statements as to what is typical at
various ages.

Random Scribbling

There are developmental stages in the scribbling
process. Although a casual observer may not be able
to distinguish between the scribbles made by a two
year old and a three year old, or in some cases even a
four year old, definite differences exist. The first stage
of development, disordered or *random scribbling,*
starts at about one year of age, and lasts until two or
two and a half. Actually, it is not random at all, but
only appears this way to an adult. Instead, this scrib-

11. *A preschooler's random scribbling is actually very purposeful drawing. Notice how the drawing tool is held between the fingers.*

bling is composed of definite lines made with simple movements. The drawing instrument is usually gripped tightly in the fingers, and the wrist does not move very much. The swing of the arm back and forth determines the direction and length of the lines; these are typically repeated several times. The youngster often watches closely to see what he is doing, but apparently the importance of watching is to follow and enjoy the lines, not to control them; yet sometimes he looks away while continuing to scribble. The drawing is a record of motor coordination, with lines

usually curving in a semicircular pattern toward the body, or up and down lines if the elbow is bent. The drawing tool is rarely taken from the paper except at the end of these sweeps. Later, as the wrist becomes more flexible, smaller arcs will be made, but there is still little movement in the fingers. Part of the reason is that the grip on the pencil or crayon tends to vary; sometimes the youngster will hold the drawing instrument as if it were a hammer, and at other times grasp it tightly between his fingers.

A study of the collected drawings made by a French child from 16 to 21 months of age (Lurcat, 1962) indicates how the direction of the scribbles evolves from the back and forth movements of the whole arm to a gradual increase in the rotation of the forearm, with curves and loops appearing as the wrist motion develops. The characteristics of this stage are basically the result of motor development, the development of the physical foundations for drawing and writing.

Many children have gone through the random scribbling stage before arriving in a nursery school setting. This sounds a little as if the stage disappears

12. (*Above*) *This scribble by a two and a half year old child shows how the arm movements push the crayon in arcs across the page.*

13. *Now the scribble shows greater control and concentration of lines in certain areas. This was drawn by a three and a half year old.*

overnight, which of course is not so. Each stage of development builds upon the previous one, and no stage ever really disappears. But it does appear that the random scribbling process is a first step for all children in developing their ability to control the marking tool and to put marks only where they are wanted.

Controlled Scribbling

The next stage of development, *controlled scribbling*, lasts about a year. Actually the child's drawings do not look very different. However, now instead of the scribbles being primarily a result of the physical action of the hand pushing and pulling the pencil across the paper, the child appears to have visual control over where the marks occur. In the beginning stage, a child may look away while scribbling, whereas now one often finds a youngster's nose almost glued to the paper as the scribble is formed, watching carefully as he draws. Controlled scribbling includes a wider range of scribbles and more intricate patterns of loops and swirls than is included with the larger muscle movements of the two year old. The wrist is now more flexible, and often the drawing instrument is held in a fashion closer to the usual adult grip. The marks are made mostly on the paper instead of occasionally wandering off, and sometimes certain parts of the paper get a good deal of attention. In drawing, there seems to be no compulsion about filling the paper, but when youngsters paint, it sometimes becomes a challenge to cover the whole piece of paper as if the child were painting the side of a house.

Greater control over the materials is needed for painting than for using fiber-tipped pen, crayon, or pencil. The big brush, the fluid paint that needs to be transferred from container to paper, and the sometimes nearly vertical position of the painting surface, all require a more complete mastery of the process. This means that controlled scribbling continues for a longer time with painting than with more easily controlled materials. Recalling some of our observations

14. *Scribbling usually lasts longer in painting than in drawing. This nursery school child is working on a flat surface, which makes the paint easier to control.*

in the nursery school, it seemed that the mere task of putting each color on the paper was a challenge.

Goertz (1966) tried having 48 youngsters from 16 months to 58 months of age scribble both with a marking ballpoint pen and with one that left no mark. She hypothesized that children under two would not notice that the one pen made no mark, but she found that all children, even the youngest ones, spent more time drawing with the pen that made a mark. Very young children, although they did scribble with the nonmarking pen, soon gave up. Older children of three or four quickly pointed out that the pen left no mark and wanted another one. In looking over her data, Goertz also found that children with a lot of drawing experience and parental interest seemed to exhibit slightly advanced drawing behavior. Many of the children were met in their own homes; the parents expressed widely differing reactions to having their children scribble, from the one extreme of a mother who questioned the value of this activity to that of a mother who provided available materials and constant encouragement. There is not enough evidence to show that children who draw a lot actually develop faster in their drawing abilities, but available evidence in related fields gives support to this assumption. This whole topic will be discussed in more detail in Chapter 9.

Naming of Scribbling

Sometime around the age of three and a half or four, children begin to give names to the marks they are making. It takes a pretty good stretch of the imagination for adults to recognize the cat scratching or the knee hurting in the scribbles that are made. The child may not actually start a drawing with subject matter in mind, but the marks often connote some meaning to the youngster which gives him thought for further scribbles. There has been some speculation as to whether these marks are indeed intended to be representations of objects; they certainly do not seem to be visual representations. However, there is no doubt

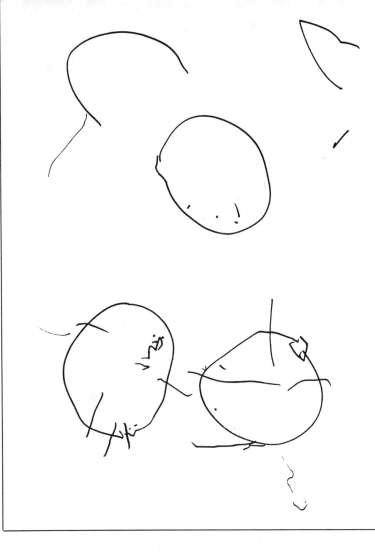

15. *These scribbles may actually represent people. A closed form with appended lines is repeated several times.*

in the child's mind that the naming of these marks defines them clearly, for himself and any observer who happens to be nearby. The serious intent with which children draw makes it obvious that these marks are very important and should be treated with respect.

Our observations indicated that the meaning a child may have given to some of his scribbles could change as more lines were put down or as his thoughts moved from one topic to another. The naming of these scribbles illustrates an important step in the development of abstract thought; essentially the children are now able to see relationships between the marks they make on the paper and objects or events in their experience. It indicates a shift away from the mere physical control over the lines to an understanding of these lines as symbols that stand for things or have similar qualities to things the child knows. Possibly the identification of these qualities, the up and down line for running or the wiggly line at the bottom of the paper for water, can give us some indication of the manner in which a child categorizes various segments of experience, how a child understands these relationships within a common framework. How this relationship is established or what essential feature of the drawing signifies this reference is sometimes not easy for an adult to understand. But the child's excitement at this discovery of the relationship is easily understood.

Early Representational Attempts

It usually is after the age of four that children's drawings begin to look more like the object that is supposed to be represented. It is sometimes uncertain whether the child decided that this particular drawing is going to represent a man, or whether the scribbles and lines and circles that are drawn accidentally appear to represent a man. Earlier scribbles and marks might very well be representations of things around the child, but not just visual representations; instead kinesthetic or tactile sensations may be shown. If you were to close your eyes and try to draw a blanket just from the sense of touch, it might look surprisingly like the scribbles of a three year old. It is a wonderful feeling to be able to talk to a child at the *early represen-tational stage* of development about recognizable subject matter in his art, particularly after many months of frustration at not being able to understand what all those marks were about.

In a study conducted at Brandeis University (Golomb, 1974) of young children's representations of a human figure in drawing and in clay modeling, it was found that at times children conjured up fantastic stories, only minimally related to the forms they have produced. This was found true for scribbles as well; sometimes these fantasies were also used by older children to rationalize why their drawings seemed distorted.

16. *Drawings are not always attempts at representation. This scribbler has good control over his tool; notice the adult grip.*

Since most adults assume that pictures are visual representations of our environment, there is the natural assumption that young children's drawings are attempts at visual representations too. It is thought that the reason that three year olds cannot draw readily recognizable objects is because they lack motor control, or perceptual awareness, or a combination of these. However, there seems to be some indication that the three year old may be drawing his experiences with objects rather than attempting to portray a camera-like reproduction of the form he sees.

Several objects were taken into the nursery school for children to draw. These were three-dimensional

17. *Sometimes it seems that the child really has struggled to represent something. It is easy to guess that this is a person.*

geometric forms with open ends and holes in one or more sides. Each youngster was able to examine and manipulate these geometric forms and then was asked to draw these with a felt-tipped pen on white paper. The drawings ranged from scribbles to a fair representation of the object. Of particular interest were those drawings which had a vague relationship to the geometric form. Some children drew only those parts of the form which they touched. For example, a round hole that one youngster felt around with his finger was drawn quite large and isolated from the rest of the drawing. In another instance, the open ends of a cylinder were drawn with vague lines connecting the two ends. The distortion in these drawings apparently resulted from the child's experience with part of the object, and did not represent how the object appeared.

The child's visual awareness of the environment begins to play an important part during this stage of early representation, because he now has the ability to *recall* visual images. This is different from the ability to *recognize* similarities or to be aware of some relationship between what was drawn and some object or action. Now the child is able to reproduce at will a symbol for an object, although not a likeness. Gradually the drawings and paintings will take on a closer relationship to nature. However, these representations have little in common with what adults consider the real world. Heads that seem nothing more than circles with two dangling lines for legs seem enough to signify a person for most children. It would be amusing to think that children actually see people as two long legs with a head on top, really perceiving people as

18. *This is a typical head-feet representation of a man. As drawn by a four year old, it serves as a quick symbol for a person.*

closed forms walking around in fairly undifferentiated backgrounds. A better explanation would be that the child is not trying to make a copy of a person, but is using the head-feet representation as a symbol for a person. He is not trying to draw the world as it is, but has a shorthand method which he has created to stand for objects. However, this head-feet symbol is so common among young children everywhere that one wonders if it is almost preprogrammed at birth.

Another possible explanation of the head-feet representation is that the youngster is actually making a visual representation of himself. If we gaze forward, generally all we can see of ourselves are arms sticking out as if from our heads, and our legs protruding beneath us. Adults trying to make an accurate drawing of what they see of themselves would make a similar type of head-feet drawing. Children might be merely representing their perception of self rather than representing an impression of another person.

Or possibly this head-feet representation is actually what the child knows about himself and is not at all a representation of what he sees. The head is obviously the important part of the body since this is where the talking and eating takes place. The eyes, nose, mouth, and ears make the head the center of sensory activity; by adding legs to make it mobile, and adding arms for feeding or grasping, we have a truly functional being. At any rate, we must be careful not to assume that, just because we as adults see a recognizable form emerging, young children are now attempting to draw naturalistically, and that these drawings are poor imitations of the real world and need to be corrected.

In addition to people, objects appear in these early drawings, objects that are meaningful and close to the child. These include pets, a house, and even trees or flowers that the child may have touched or handled. However, landscape drawings, still lifes, representations of shade or shadow, or interesting patterns of branches against the sky never appeared in the drawings we have collected.

There seems to be no portrayal of space in these drawings. The two-dimensional surface of the paper is not violated; there is no attempt to make some objects seem further away than others, or to indicate three dimensionality. Rather, objects are placed on the paper in what seems a random fashion. Each object or person is portrayed as a separate entity as if the child is drawing first this, and then this, and then that. Within a drawing of an object, parts seem to be located in relation to one another. That is, the eyes and mouth of a person may be properly located within the head, with legs beneath, but another figure will be drawn floating above or below the first, with seemingly no relationship between them. We were not able to find overlapping except within the object itself, and even there it was rare. Usually the arms of a figure were drawn projecting straight out from the head, with the fingers extending still further, rather than having these parts overlapping. The drawings seem more like the addition of successive symbols rather than an organized coherent portrayal of objects relating to each other.

Frequently the space available helped determine the shape of the house or man. The drawing varied to take advantage of the empty spaces on the paper, and

19. *Valerie shows herself dancing. Notice the extended fingers and the interesting use of space.*

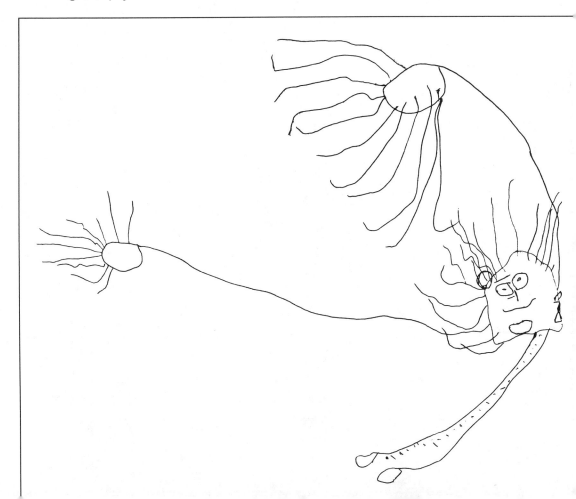

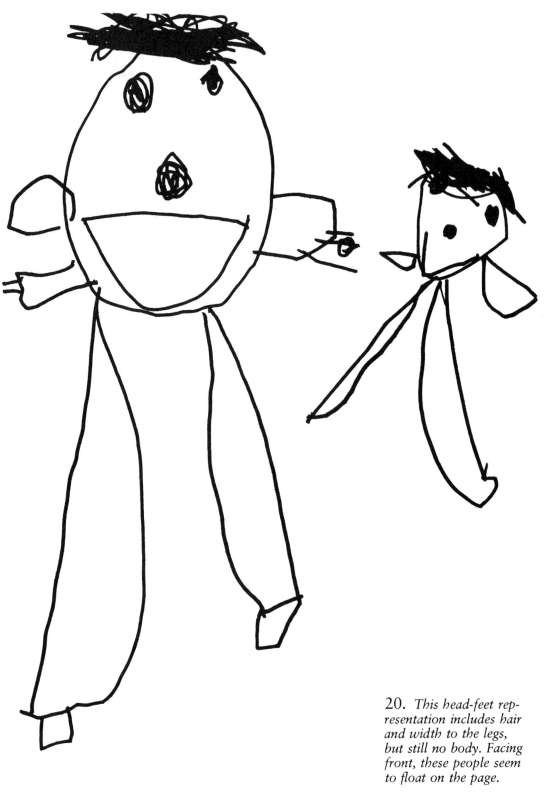

20. *This head-feet representation includes hair and width to the legs, but still no body. Facing front, these people seem to float on the page.*

the symbol for anything was not so rigid that it could not be distorted or drawn so as to fit. At times the paper would be turned around to bring the empty space closer and handier to work on, so the finished picture appears to show houses inverted and people standing on their heads.

Each of the objects is drawn facing forward. It is as if the child drew the person looking directly at him, and the drawing looks directly back, not at other things in the picture. Even the door on a house is conveniently located on the front, somewhat like a stage set waiting for the child himself to open it.

It is somewhat difficult to talk of exaggeration of parts, in the sense that one part, such as the hands, might be drawn out of proportion to the rest of a person. This assumes that there is an attempt on the part of the child at representing a figure in proportion, but this is not an accurate assessment of what the child is doing. We are often amused by cartoons or caricatures drawn by adults; exaggeration of characteristics plays a key role in recognition of certain characters, particularly in the political arena. We realize that the cartoonist is not attempting to make a photographic likeness but to make a certain point. Children don't seem to be attempting a photographic likeness either. What we see as distortion is not seen by children as distortion in their own drawings. Sometimes four year olds will talk about the funny man they drew, but it is *not* a funny drawing. There are no excuses made for the large hands or small legs although there may be an explanation of why the hands are large or legs are small; from a child's point of view, nothing is wrong with the drawing itself. He brings a picture into existence and it represents what he thinks it does, not what the viewer would like to think it should. It does not stand for something else; it is just his picture.

Preschematic Drawing

By the time a child is five we again see changes developing in his mode of drawing. Although it is important to note that these changes happen slowly

21. *This drawing by a five year old includes a body; but the head, body, feet, and even the hands with many fingers are merely closed circular shapes.*

and somewhat erratically and that individual children progress at different rates, there are some important differences between drawings by children of four and by those of five years of age. Objects do not seem to float in space quite as much. Now there is a right-side-up; we begin to see a line that stands for the sky, and a line that stands for the ground. This base for the objects to rest on grows stronger as the youngster grows older. It begins to make its appearance as a definite base line by about the age of six, and usually continues as a drawing method for most children for the next few years.

With a greater feeling for order in the drawings by five year olds, there comes a greater understanding of the relative sizes of the objects portrayed. Mommy and Daddy are often drawn bigger, although inanimate objects are still relatively small and usually devoid of detail. But the greatest change seems to come in the representation of the human figure. The head-feet representation no longer suffices. There is now a body, usually with arms coming from it rather than from the head, and with fingers, though not always the right number. There are legs, usually drawn with double lines to suggest volume, with some indication of feet, shoes, or even toes shown. Hair is often included, and some indication of clothing.

Each child seems to develop his own method of drawing a person; it seems almost as if each youngster were trying several different ways of portraying a person before he develops his own formula. This flexibility is the reason this stage of development is called the *preschematic* stage (Lowenfeld and Brittain, 1975). Often the body is some geometric shape — a circle, square, or triangle — and the head, arms, and legs are

22. *By six years, most children will begin to set the elements in their pictures on a base line. However, the drawing of a person is still made up of geometric forms.*

attached to it. These parts are usually not recognizable as body parts if viewed apart from the whole. In fact, we have no drawings that depict only a part of the body, no isolated arm holding something, no mouth open ready to eat, and no drawing of just the upper body. It is as if the youngster must draw the whole person, either to communicate the concept of person, or else because he is unable to consider a detail separated from the whole.

The five year old does not seem to have as much difficulty with paints as does the four year old, and there are fewer mechanical paintings. By this we mean that fewer paintings look as if they were the result of picking up the brush and applying paint above the jar in the easel trough. Now there are objects and people painted, usually one to a piece of paper, and often filling all of the available space. Color almost appears to be incidental. A man can be painted with a blue outline, or red; it seems to make little difference. Whatever paint is available will do. A mass of color is used at times, but this seems related more to painting a surface than to portraying something. In a sense, the children draw with the paint brush and leave the outline as the finished picture. There has been speculation that color usage bears some relation to the mood or psychological state of the child as he paints. However, from our observations and from a close look at the paintings themselves, we would dismiss that possibility. There does seem to be a tendency to use colors that contrast with the background and surface; that is, when children are given a dark piece of paper, they use the whites and yellows more. But for the most part children seem to paint with what is available to them.

Stages in Clay

The clay products also reflect development. At two years of age a child will beat the clay, pull it apart, and mush it together. When the child is three, the clay gets formed into balls — sometimes quite a few balls — and rolled into long snake-like shapes. By

23. *This three year old is making clay balls, lots of clay balls, and is proud of the accomplishment.*

age four the child puts these balls together to make somewhat more complex forms, and holes may be punched in a form or parts pulled out. These are often given names in much the same way that scribbles are named. But the five year old sometimes announces what he is going to make and sets about making it.

24. *Just as we have seen head-feet drawings by young children, we also find head-feet representations made out of clay.*

25. *Sometimes the snake-like forms of clay that children make are used as lines to create a person in outline, in much the same way as a person is made in a drawing.*

There are as many variations in the molded forms as in the drawn or painted forms.

For some children the clay is used to outline forms, with snake-like shapes being substituted for drawn lines; these are arranged on a flat surface so that the finished product appears in relief rather than as a free-standing piece of sculpture. The features can be added within the doughnut hole space for the face, or drawn with a finger or other tool into a flattened cookie-like head. Arms and legs are added with flattened strips, so that the end results are similar to those drawn or painted. A few free-standing shapes

26. Here we see clay used three-dimensionally, with parts added to a body to make a person.

were made; some of these were men that started out like snowmen. There are some good reasons for this use of clay. Constructing a human figure from clay is a difficult task for adults, and sculptors use various devices, such as armatures, to hold the clay form erect. The solution of making a figure flat seems to be a good one. There was no indication of abstract thought portrayed in these sculptured forms by five year olds: no tall forms with negative space, no purposeful putting together various-sized pieces, and no graceful arcs or seeming concern for aesthetic values that adults might strive toward.

Much more could be said about the work saved for our art collection. Many of our additional comments were somewhat more intuitive in nature. For example, most of the drawings were a pleasure to look at; there was a freshness and directness which was very appealing. Arms are outstretched, smiles are everywhere, colors are bright; the art seems spontaneous and uninhibited. However, several questions were raised about the value of art experiences, how children learn, and the optimum conditions for creative growth. These gave rise to more controlled studies which will be discussed in the following chapters.

3

Relevance of Stages in Art

Studying the Process of Development

Our examination of the drawings, paintings, and clay products of young children made it possible to note the differences in the ways that children create and in the art they produce. However, merely noting the differences does not explain why these differences exist. Intriguing questions crossed the minds of the investigators. Does the child see the world in ways different from adults? Does the child need to be taught a vocabulary of art? To what extent is art a natural unfolding process which is predetermined? Is it easier for children to copy simple forms than it is for them to create forms from their understanding of the environment? What other aspects of behavior are parallel to

47

developments in art? Can development be accelerated? The list of questions seemed almost endless.

In observing the creative behavior of children in nursery schools and kindergartens, it was evident that art is only one aspect of their activity, and it cannot be separated from their total behavior. These are the same children who struggle to remove coats, watch fish in the aquarium, enjoy snacks with other children, grow restless when books are read to them, or become upset when someone else gets to the tricycle first. Their creative activities reflect and contribute to their thoughts and actions. It is no wonder that drawings and paintings are sometimes used as measures of intelligence and are examined for evidence of personality disorders.

As children develop, they deal with creative experiences in predictable ways. The art products we gathered document these changes. Drawings were particularly useful since they could be readily compared, and seemed to reflect a child's thinking more directly than when a child was confronted with art materials that were more difficult to control. The previous chapter dealt with some of the differences we saw in the products, but there were also discernible differences in the process itself.

During the process of collecting drawings from children younger than two years of age, graduate student investigators made comments that bear repeating. None of these young children needed to be told how to use the drawing instruments provided for them. Although at first a fifteen month old child enjoyed chewing the crayon, making marks on a paper ended up as a more worthwhile pursuit. The motions of the scribbling activity seemed to be pleasurable for very young children, and they were not concerned if the marks occasionally wandered off the sheet of paper. These same children also enjoyed other physical sensations such as being bounced on an adult's knees, feeling the texture of a fur coat, or running the zipper on one of the graduate students' jackets up and down. It may be that only through physical exploration can the environment make sense to children of this age. These children did not name their drawings, nor were they particularly aware of what they had done. When they used paint, the sticky quality and the flapping of the

27. A group activity, such as music and clapping, may not involve all children to the same extent.

brush on the paper seemed satisfying. These art activities lasted for only a brief period before the child would tire and look elsewhere for amusement.

The two year olds who were observed began to pay attention to the marks they were making. They were also much more particular about the color of crayon selected, whereas the younger children would pick any color. It appeared that contrast with the drawing surface had now become important. A careful examination of young children was undertaken by Holladay (1966), who studied 64 children from two to five years of age. These children did a number of drawing tasks and copied figures and lines using crayons of different values. Holladay also kept a record of the length of time children of various ages spent drawing, noting the type of grip used, and determining the amount of pressure children applied by

28. *Painting a paper bag may not be particularly interesting to an adult, but try holding the brush between the fingers this way.*

having them draw on pressure-sensitive paper. Holladay's study makes it possible to describe what is typical of a two, three, four, and five year old.

The two year old grasps the drawing instrument in a number of different ways: like a hammer, between the fingers, with an overhand grip, or some variation of these. The fingers and wrist do not flex, and the paper is likely to flip around since the free hand is not used to steady the paper. The two year old typically spends less than a minute on each drawing, and these drawings are scribbled with no concern about filling the paper or drawing in any particular area.

The three year old is able to steady the paper with his free hand, and he spends twice as long drawing as the two year old. He grasps the drawing tool in ways closer to how an adult might, and the drawings contain a greater variety of marks, with attention now paid to filling the paper and massing scribbles together in what seems to be a more purposeful way.

The four year old has pretty well mastered the usual adult finger grip, and he spends an average of two and a half minutes on a crayon drawing. He seems to have physical control over his medium using increased finger and wrist motion. The child chooses his crayons for particular purposes although the colors selected seem to bear no relationship to any representational content. Although scribbles predominate, some representational drawings do appear, especially by girls. The scribbles seem to be more like designs which are often balanced across the page, with certain parts getting a good deal of attention.

By the age of five, the youngster seems to have complete control over the drawing tool. The grip is the normal adult one, and marks on the paper vary in length, direction, and pressure. The average time spent drawing continues to increase, and now a greater percentage of children make drawings with some representational theme. The lines drawn are primarily outlines of shapes or objects, with boys especially continuing to make patterns and designs over the drawing surface. Probably one of the most important aspects of Holladay's study is that he has established that a child's motor control of both pressure and direction in the act of drawing is quite well established

by the time representational symbols appear. As early as the age of three most children make scribbles which show a high degree of awareness of space, filling of particular areas, balance on the sheet of paper, and a stabilized line quality; these are basically compositional qualities and might even be construed as the beginnings of an aesthetic awareness. But Holladay points out that the balanced quality of drawings no longer seems as important to the child when he begins to draw more from a communicational point of view, that is, when representational symbols appear.

Our observations indicate that children can be quite pleased with some of their art products by the age of three. Prior to that time it appears that the drawing act is sufficient in itself; children will sometimes walk away from a painting or drawing as if the task is complete and it is time to start on something else. However, at about three it seems that the children become aware of their own competence and can even be amazed at the nice job they have done by filling the paper with paint or by using colored felt-tipped pens. It is at this point that children enjoy showing their products to adults, and the "Look at what I made" eager child shows the picture to the nursery school teacher who usually responds with an automatic "Isn't that nice."

Other Classifications

29. *"Look what I made!" No teacher has to hand out praise when a child discovers her own abilities.*

Although some adults may not be interested in the scribbles that young children make, a few have looked closely at this period of art expression. One rather elaborate system of classifying children's early drawings was made by Kellogg (1969). She gathered thousands of children's drawings from a nursery school and analyzed them in terms of the basic forms that she saw evolving. These basic forms included the dot, the vertical line, the horizontal line, the diagonal line, the curved line, multiple lines, zigzags, loops, circles, crosses, and so forth. According to Kellogg, twenty scribbles are combined in various ways to make up the nursery school child's drawings; a key

Manuel

part of the sequence is apparently the development of the Mandala, a circle divided into quarters by a cross. This is seen as the basis for representing the sun, flowers, humans, and so forth. However, when we examined the drawings we collected from nursery schools and kindergartens, in general we did not find these basic forms being used by children. Kellogg also implies that prehistoric art followed this same evolutionary pattern and that the art of prehistoric man utilized the very same symbols that are found in the art of young children today. However, there is little basis for this assumption, as we shall see in Chapter 6.

Other writers in the area of children's art (Jameson, 1968; McFee, 1970; Lansing, 1970) have classified the art of preschool children into basically the same developmental patterns mentioned in Chapter 2,

30. *Children from all parts of the world begin drawing in similar ways. Here is a drawing by a Brazilian boy.*

from the earliest marks which primarily result from motor or physical manipulation, to the appearance of recognizable objects at about the age of four and a half or five. Sometimes these stages in children's art are called other names: scribbling may be called the manipulative stage, or head-feet representation may be called tadpole drawing (not because it is an attempt at making tadpoles, but because the drawing of a man resembles one, with a circle for a head with appendages).

Young children throughout the world seem to

31. *This is a drawing by a child in Pakistan. Cultural influences do not disguise the fact that this is a child's drawing.*

32. *Here is a drawing by a child in Micronesia. Some cultural differences can be seen, but the way people are drawn looks familiar.*

follow the same stages in artistic development. Our examination of drawings by children from other countries (Pakistan, Brazil, Egypt, India, Uruguay, Japan, and many European countries) indicates that these early forms of art production are similar for all children. Differences seem more related to the materials used than to any cultural differences.

Writing and Drawing

Preliminary observations of children's drawings suggested that those children who could write their names were also children who had progressed beyond

33. *The line quality in this drawing is reflected in the attempt at name writing at the top of the page.*

the scribbling stage in drawing. In other words, there seemed to be a parallel development between the achievement of forms in drawing and achievement of forms in writing. To test this idea, an experiment was undertaken.

Several drawings were gathered from each of forty preschool children over a period of two weeks. Each child was asked to put his name on his drawing, and if he said he could not do this task, he was given encouragement or told that he could make believe he was writing his name. The drawings and attempts at writing were compared on about 100 drawings on which both appeared. Only those drawings were examined in which the drawing instrument used was the same for both drawing and writing. The results were quite clear; if a child makes closed forms in drawings, his writing also includes closed forms. If the child is still scribbling on the paper, the writing sample, although smaller, is also primarily a scribble. Those

34. *Kinga's writing shows development comparable to her drawing. By the time children make recognizable objects in their drawings, they are also interested in shaping letters.*

children who make recognizable objects in their draw-ings also make recognizable letters. The few excep-tions may have been motivational.

Although this study was relatively simple, the re-sults clearly supported the hypothesis, and no further plans were made to enlarge the sample or repeat the experiment. It became obvious to the investigators that the production of forms should be parallel in both drawing and writing. The implications of this take on some importance in the teaching of writing. Some children at the kindergarten level will not be making forms that are closed, or naming that which they have made, or even making recognizable objects in their drawings. Writing exercises would be beyond the abilities of these youngsters and could be frustrat-ing. Since there seem to be ample differences between the size of the drawing and the writing (even the youngest children made the writing much smaller), it would appear that problems of muscle control or coordination are not the prime factors in achieving success in writing. However, the ability to form con-cepts and portray recognizable objects seems basic to both methods of form making.

Children's Responses to Directions

The work of art becomes communication when symbols appear. These symbols seem not as much an opportunity to communicate with peers or adults as to communicate with one's self. It was observed that children occasionally talked while painting, but not to anyone in particular, and almost as if talking to the objects that were being drawn. Art in the adult world is often considered a means of communication, but young children's art has not been viewed in this con-text. An intriguing question to be examined might be the relationship between speech and drawing as these develop in the preschool child.

An investigation into the relationship between the stages of scribbling and how children respond to com-munications from adults was carried out by Clarke (1974). Her work was based in part on some of the theories of the Soviet psychologist, A. R. Luria. Clarke's population consisted of 81 children from three to six years of age. After some preliminary discussion with each child during which rapport was established, it was ascertained that the children understood the terms to be used. Each child was then given a stick, and the experimenter picked a ring from a pile on the table and instructed each child to "put it on." After the child had put several rings on the stick in this fashion, the instructions were changed to "don't put it on." The entire procedure was repeated; the child first was asked to put the rings on and then, once this action was well established, the child was told not to put the next one on. Scoring was relatively simple because most children either complied with the changed commands or ignored them. Some children realized there was a change in the directions, hesitated, but then continued; some children said the commands over to themselves as if coaching themselves in what they should be doing. It was assumed that the children who ignored the directive functions of speech and continued in the motor activity of putting the rings on the stick would be in the scribbling stage. It was further hypothesized that children who could use these verbal signals to direct their own motor activities would also be able to direct their own motor activities while drawing and would be in the naming of scribbling stage. This in fact was what Clarke found out. There was a positive relationship between the child's ability to respond to directions and the developmental level of the child's scribbles ($r = .62$). It is possible that the same causal factors influence behavior in both areas; that is, the inability of children to stop perseverated motions on command may be reflected in scribbling behavior since this is also a motor activity. When the child begins to name these scribbles and have control over the lines so that they are no longer disordered or randomly distributed across the paper, the child can also control his own movements by stopping and starting actions upon request.

Some of the implications of this relationship can be seen in the way young children perform a variety of activities in the nursery school. For example, often an elaborate pasting exercise is planned by the teacher; but the children become involved in the act of

35. *Sometimes paste, with its sticky consistency, can be more fun than the project planned by the teacher.*

pasting itself. Three year olds may paste one piece of paper after another without any concern about placing these in some sort of pattern on another sheet of paper. Sometimes pasting becomes so absorbing that the child will leave the activity without any product to show for the work except for the spreading of the paste. In one of our videotapes, a sequence shows a girl who has just mastered the task of cutting with a pair of scissors. She forgot why the cutting process was important, and simply concentrated on the motor activity of cutting. Any mother of a three year old child can certainly testify to the enjoyment a small child gets in using a sponge to clean a table. Cleaning with the sponge and squishing the water is an activity in itself, and the purpose of cleaning up is often lost.

Comparing Clay with Drawing

The same stages of development as seen in drawings exist in working with clay as discussed in Chapter 2. The first experience with clay seems to be primarily tactile, with the two year old sticking his finger into the clay, squeezing it, or breaking pieces off, but not attempting to make it into a particular shape. It is not until the child is five that the name of an object comes before it is made.

However, drawing lines on a two-dimensional surface to express the characteristics of a three-dimensional world may be seen as a more difficult process. It calls for a degree of abstraction which might be difficult for a young child to achieve. Therefore clay, being already three-dimensional, might actually be the easiest material for representation. A study was undertaken to determine whether clay would facilitate a more advanced type of representation than drawing.

One of the local nursery schools served as the experimental population. Examples were gathered of the clay modeling and drawings by these children. Each child was motivated individually; half the children were asked to do the drawing, and the other half were asked to model with clay. The directions were quite simple: "I want you to make a picture of a man. You know what a man is. Your Daddy is a man. Make the very best picture that you can. Take your time and work very carefully. And be sure to make the whole man, not just the head." When the child was finished, he was asked to identify parts that were not clear, so such questions as, "Tell me about your picture," or "What might that be?" were asked. Two days later the same study was repeated except that now each child who had drawn before was given a ball of clay and those who had worked with clay now drew.

The products of these 17 children included in the study were examined. It was possible to give a numerical score to the drawings based on the Goodenough-Harris Draw-A-Man Scale (Harris, 1963); an adaptation of this scale was used to rate the clay products, which were a little more difficult to score. However, the drawings as a whole did get higher scores. As a check, three judges were asked to rate the pictures and clay models according to the degree of accuracy in representation. The judges agreed at a surprising .01 level of confidence. Again, the drawings were rated higher; no piece of clay work was judged higher than any drawing, although in some cases they rated equally high. Therefore, it would seem that clay does not provide the opportunity for children to express their environment more easily than a drawing does.

There were several things that resulted from this study besides the comparison of drawing and clay work. If there was no indication of a man in the drawing, there was no indication of a man in the clay work. Apparently, if a child cannot make a figure in a two-dimensional medium, he cannot do so in clay either. Also, a number of children attempted to use the clay in a two-dimensional fashion; that is, some children rolled little snakes of clay and with these constructed a two-dimensional man on a flat surface rather than modeling a man in an expected three-dimensional way. The three-dimensional structures suffered a little when children placed one lump of clay on top of another, but, for the most part, one could still see the intent of the child. In both the drawing and the clay work, it appeared that these children were really not constructing a visual representation of a man, and the child's thinking process was the same

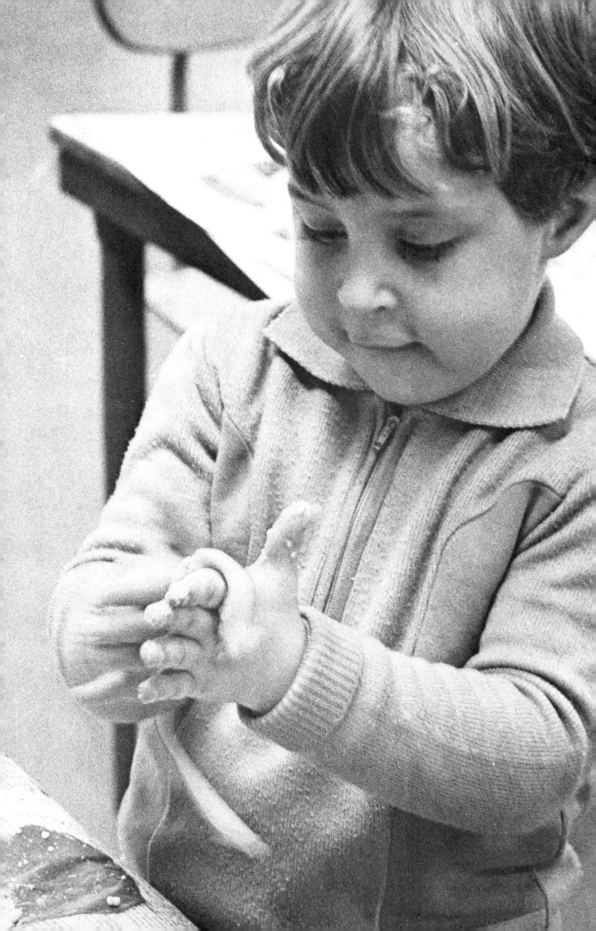

in both art forms. One big advantage in drawing was that every line put down by the child remained until the drawing was completed. Working in clay, however, meant that parts became distorted as the shape itself was manipulated. Probably filming the process of working with clay would be a more satisfactory approach to the problem.

While working with clay, one child got quite frustrated because the forms he had called legs did not want to stick to the body shape. This same child was also frustrated in making his drawing, complained that it didn't look right, and asked for another sheet of paper. For this child, the material itself was not the key factor in his inability to make the intended forms. However, other materials might be easier to manipulate than clay, and further work on this question was felt important.

Differences in Development

Seeing the developmental changes that take place in children's art within the span of a few years, it is easy to speculate that these changes are not only universal in nature but also are inborn. That is, since these changes go from random scribbling, in which the child is developing control over his drawing instrument at the age of two, to sophisticated symbols for his environment and rather complete control over his drawing instrument at the age of six, it is tempting to suggest that these changes are sequential and are merely a result of maturation. However, there is enough evidence from our observations and from the study of children's drawings to indicate that this may not be entirely true.

There does seem to be enough evidence from our studies to indicate that all children pass through comparable stages of development. The scribbles come before the head-feet representation, and the rather random distribution of objects in space comes before an organization of space on the page with a baseline at the bottom. The general configuration comes before attention is focused upon details, and outline drawing

36. Being able to make long snakes of clay is no simple task. These snakes were later used as lines to make a man.

37. *A simple outline is enough to give the impression of this five year old being in the rain protected by a raincoat.*

is universally applicable as a means of portraying parts of the environment. However, all children do not arrive at the same point at the same time. We have seen some three year olds who are drawing in ways comparable to the normal four year old. We have also observed children who at the age of five are drawing like four year olds. Obviously something either genetically- or environmentally-based must have caused these deviations from the norm. If the sequence is predetermined, the time intervals are not.

We found that children who enjoy making art products tend to do this better than children who do not seem to enjoy these activities. Enjoyment was indicated by the length of time children spent drawing and painting or working with clay. This should not be considered unusual, for adults also tend to be better at those activities on which they spend time. However, one wonders whether it is the time spent at these activities that makes them seem more worthwhile to the children and in turn makes their products more advanced for their age, or whether it is the satisfaction in the products that keeps the child at the activity for a longer period of time.

Whatever the reason, it is clear that some children produce works of art that are well above the norm, whereas other children either are unable to do this or have not had the experience that allows this to happen. Waiting for these children to catch up is the usual method in nursery school and kindergarten; our observations indicate that most teachers tend to be reluctant to help children in their artwork. These same teachers did not seem to be hesitant to encourage

38. This kindergarten youngster's drawing is a profile, which is unusual. Note the awareness of clothing and even the hat, with a pinwheel on top.

children to identify shapes, copy forms, or to look at and name colors, nor did they feel inhibited about encouraging children to speak in full sentences, use the proper tense, or develop skills in counting. We observed some teachers who provided models for children to follow or had particular skills that they wanted children to develop in the arts, such as cutting, tearing, pasting, or using the brush and dipping it in the paint in some prescribed manner. For the most part, children were bored by this type of lesson, and little in the way of carryover could be found once the exercise was over. Possibly the kind of exercises designed by the teacher to increase the child's competency in the arts did not provide learning experiences that had meaning to the youngster involved. If the end product does not have much significance for the young child, focusing on a particular skill necessary to produce it apparently has little influence on his retaining any of the abilities taught, nor does it facilitate improvement in the child's developmental level. This is not to suggest that developmental levels are iron-clad, but it does suggest that focusing on the particular skill necessary for a particular task is not the efficient way of developing a youngster's competency or interest in the arts.

One of the most important considerations relative to developmental levels is the evidence that a child thinks in ways different from adults. He is not a miniature adult who needs to have information and processing skills fed into him; rather, the developmental levels indicate that the child understands the world and acts upon this understanding in ways that may seem foreign to adult thinking. There are many psychologists who have spent time examining the process of thinking. One of the most well known is Jean Piaget.

Although Piaget has not been directly concerned with children's drawings and paintings except for some copying abilities, he and his colleagues provide an interesting format or framework for understanding the changes that go on in the process of thought in the young child (Piaget, 1955; Piaget and Inhelder, 1967, 1971). They postulate four stages of cognitive development. The first is *sensory motor operations,* which lasts until the child is about 18 months of age.

The second is the *preoperational* stage, which lasts until age six or seven. The third stage is *concrete operations,* which is completed by about age eleven or twelve years. This is followed by the fourth stage, which is usually referred to as *formal operations.* Our present concern is the preoperational child who is developing the ability to manipulate symbols, who knows and understands his environment only as it can be grasped and internalized in tangible ways. Although adults might attempt a systematic approach to an art project, seeing various steps in its procedures, the young child is eager to begin to manipulate, modify and control the material in front of him. For example, an adult teacher may be concerned about the firing quality of clay, and insist that young children pull parts from the clay object rather than adding the parts to the whole, because of the possibility that air will be trapped that might destroy the object during the firing process. The young child, however, is not interested and does not understand the transformation that takes place when clay is fired. He is more interested in handling the clay and creating something from it; he probably would not recognize his own product after it was fired anyway. It is not until eleven or twelve years of age that children can understand the necessity to put clay products aside to dry or to worry about such things as air bubbles which might destroy the product in the firing.

It makes little difference whether we are looking at the behavior of a child who is doing art projects or whether we are looking at the behavior of the same child in other activities; we are still looking at the same youngster. Whatever handle we happen to use for our examinations, we are still concerned with the interaction of a child with his environment and the way a child assimilates and acts upon information. It is through this interaction process that the child acquires knowledge, adjusts his concepts of the world, and develops new patterns of expression. Without the constant contact and interaction with the environment, a child loses the stimulation and reference upon which both visual and verbal learning grow.

There is plenty of evidence in the literature that children derive pleasure from mastering tasks that have a problem-solving component. If the task is

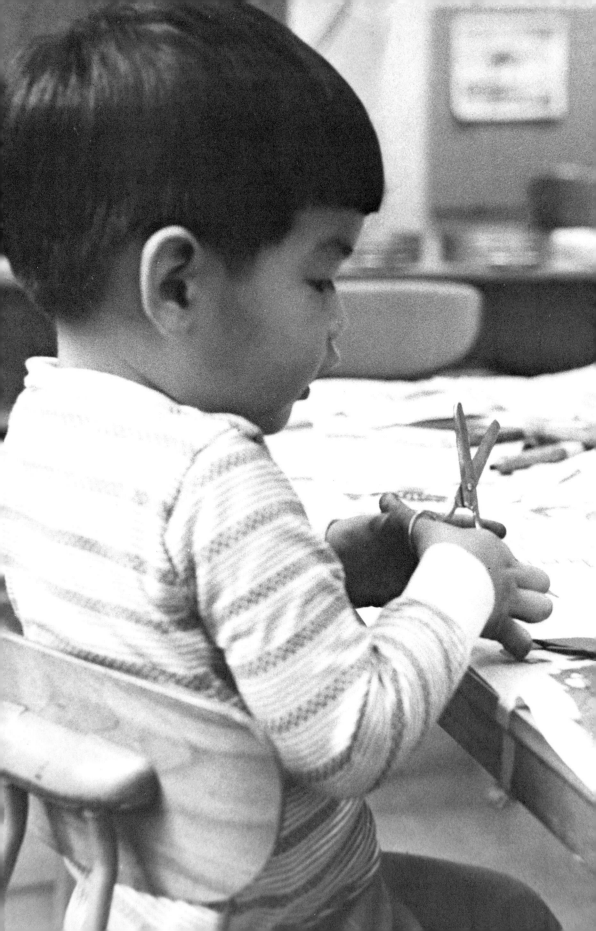

beyond the understanding of a child, for him there is actually no problem to be solved, and if the task is too simple, the mere doing of this task is boredom. Therefore, it is interesting that the challenges inherent in drawing and painting appear to evolve in a natural way to present problems that are basically intrinsic to a child's development. The arts are invariably looked upon as pleasurable, and at the same time our observations of children in nursery schools and kindergartens indicate that there is a good deal of cognitive mastery taking place. For the very young child it is a challenge to be able to use a crayon and make swirly lines over the paper, but this work is self-adjusting as the child grows older. When the scribble no longer suffices, the challenge to see the relationship between the symbol and the object becomes more important, and at each stage of development the possibility for cognitive growth exists.

39. *Just trying to figure out how scissors work can be a problem. Success sometimes comes only after much perseverance.*

4

Copying and Discrimination Ability

Controversy About Copying

It may seem remarkable that anyone should be concerned about the particular age when a child is able to copy a geometric form. However, some people have been interested in this topic, and for good reason. One of the objectives of the Head Start program has been to develop youngsters' ability to do various tasks. Since most of the children involved in Head Start programs come from so-called disadvantaged neighborhoods, it is assumed that these youngsters need to develop the same competencies as children from middle-class neighborhoods. It is suggested in the "Daily Program" for project Head Start (Caldwell, 1967) that children should be able to make circles, squares, and triangles by the time they leave the

73

program, and many ways are suggested to instruct them. Once these tasks are supposedly mastered, children are encouraged to use these geometric forms in their drawings of houses, trees, and so forth.

One of the reasons that copying abilities are stressed is that normal ages have been established for successful copying. For example, it is generally accepted that a three year old can copy a circle. By the age of four, children can usually copy a square. At about the age of five, most children can copy a triangle. But it is not until seven years of age that youngsters can successfully copy a diamond. Since most of our alphabet is based upon geometric forms, it is obvious that until some of these tasks have been achieved, it would be fruitless to try to teach any child how to copy the letters of the alphabet. Also, a child who has difficulty in copying a square by the age of four may be considered below his normal level of achievement, which can be interpreted by psychologists as meaning that the child is retarded. This will never do, so most nursery school teachers feel that teaching children how to copy geometric forms is a necessary part of their job.

In the elementary art program, children are discouraged from copying (Lowenfeld and Brittain, 1975). The rationale is related to a youngster's creativity. Since his own art products sometimes bear little resemblance to the object he is portraying, the feeling is that copying adult-made images would merely frustrate his own creative urges. If he believes that the model he is to copy is correct, then he is likely to think the one he does himself is childish and inaccurate. There is experimental evidence to support this view. Russell and Waugaman (1952) had children color in outlines of birds in a workbook. They found that 63 per cent of the children who had been thus exposed to the workbook birds lost their original visual concept of a bird, and instead tried to make a new symbol which resembled the workbook stereotype. Heilman (1954) also felt that copying and tracing were detrimental. He used some arithmetic workbooks and had children fill in the examples given; they reproduced the number of kites and stereotyped rabbits that were called for. He concluded that children can become dependent upon these workbooks

40. *Young children are exposed to numbers and letters in school, with the hope that familiarity with these symbols will encourage comprehension.*

41. (*Left*) *For children beginning formal schooling, art sometimes consists of large numbers of duplicated sheets to be dutifully colored in and graded by the teacher.*

and that the youngsters' own creative work can be seriously and negatively influenced.

The child in first grade should not have to copy a square house with a triangular roof seven times to show that he understands the meaning of the number seven. There is no evidence that a preschool child benefits from copying geometric forms such as squares and triangles in the first place. It is important to consider the negative effect of dependence upon adult concepts such as the house consisting of a triangle resting on a square. How devastating for the child who is still scribbling if the nursery school teacher

42. (*Right*) *April, who colored in the sheets for the teacher, seems very capable of producing her own drawings and paintings without the "benefit" of outlined, predetermined adult images.*

stresses the necessity of making a good looking square and thus rejects his scribbles as mistakes or uncoordinated attempts.

All of this discussion assumes that the teacher can indeed help youngsters develop the ability to copy geometric forms. Not only that, but it assumes that an adult knows enough about how children learn to be able to divide the task into teachable components, and that the youngster will be able to master the given task by following the logical sequence and practicing enough. This seems to be the way that most learning takes place, or rather this is the way that most teaching takes place. Unfortunately this method of teaching may be wrong.

In teaching a concept of geometric forms, the adult supposes that it is logical for a youngster to first learn to discriminate one form from another. That is, he should be able to find, among a series of geometric shapes, a triangle which matches the given one; or, if shown a square, he should be able to pick out another square from a series of circles, triangles, squares, and crosses. This *discrimination* seems like a relatively simple task, one which would need to be mastered before any development of copying abilities could take place.

The usual second step is that of *recognition*. This one is much more difficult since a child has to carry around with him the knowledge of what a particular geometric shape is like. Now, without having a sample to match, the youngster is asked to pick a square from a series of geometric shapes, or to identify the triangle or circle. Here the name of the shape has to be tied to a particular form, whereas in discrimination a child does not necessarily have to recall a form just from its name. Recognition is a much more difficult task.

Probably the third task in attempting to teach children how to draw geometric shapes would be exercises in *tracing*. This could be done in several ways. One method is to show a youngster a black outline of a geometric shape on a white piece of paper and have him trace over it with a transparent yellow felt marking pen. This would make visible to the child where he has made mistakes since the original geometric shape would show through the yellow line. Tracing is also one way that teachers try to develop eye-hand coordination.

The final step in this whole unfortunate procedure would be to have the youngster practice *copying* a given shape. The customary way to do this is to have a fairly large triangle drawn on one piece of paper, and to give the child a comparable blank sheet upon which he is expected to draw a triangle like the one shown. In this way he could refer to the model as often as he needed to; the model would be there for comparison. The old edict "practice makes perfect" is expected to hold true. The above procedures seem to be the method by which form copying is presently taught, but there is some evidence that this procedure is not necessarily the best way to develop copying abilities in children.

Perceptual and Motor Considerations

A study was undertaken, following the steps outlined above, to see if the inability to copy a geometric shape was caused by perceptual problems or by lack of motor ability (Collett, 1971). The subjects for this study were 48 preschool children ranging in age from three years eight months to five years seven months. There were equal numbers of boys and girls, most of them from middle-class backgrounds. Since the average four year old can already copy a square, a triangle was used for this experiment. Each youngster was asked to match a triangle to a given one in a discrimination task. Then he was told to pick out a triangle from a series of shapes as a recognition task. Next he was given a transparent yellow marker and asked to trace over a triangle. Finally he was shown a triangle and asked to copy it.

All the children were able to match a triangle with another from among the geometric figures, and all the children but one were able to pick out a triangle when asked to do so. The three year olds had difficulty in tracing a triangle, and it was also difficult for them to copy one. The correlation between these two tasks for the three year olds was high ($r = .70$).

43. *A circle is the first geometric shape copied successfully. It is usually done with one continuous line making a closed form.*

Although four and five year old children could do the tracing and copying tasks much better, there was no relationship between their ability to trace and to copy. Some five year olds could trace but not copy very well, some could copy but not trace, and some could do both. The ability to trace does not necessarily precede the ability to copy.

Discriminating one form from another and recognizing geometric shapes seemed to come fairly early; these perceptual tasks were easy for three year olds. Tracing is usually regarded as a motor ability. Although it seems logical that the development of perceptual skills and motor ability would provide the necessary basis for copying forms, this was apparently not so in the above study. Copying a form takes abilities other than merely adding together perceptual and motor skills.

We assume that the eyes, the brain, and the hand are all responsible for the copying abilities of youngsters. Yet, so far, we have only been concerned with two of these, the perceptual and the motor tasks. A child's ability to think, reason, and organize may be the most important part of the process. Since there is a definite age at which children can normally do copying tasks — a circle at three, a square at four, a triangle at about five, and a diamond at about seven years of age — then it is possible to say that this sequence of abilities may be due more to intellectual development than to either perceptual skills or motor ability.

44. *By four, most children have little difficulty copying squares. Irregularly torn wrapping paper shields the square edges of the drawing surface.*

Consequently, it is futile to try to teach children how to copy triangles or squares before they are cognitively ready.

Copying Squares

A study was undertaken to try to teach three year old children at the Cornell Nursery School how to copy squares (Brittain, 1969). Eighteen children ranging from 42 to 49 months of age were the subjects. The purpose was merely to see if the opportunity to imitate strokes, draw around square objects, trace square shapes, find squares in the environment, and so forth, would help these children in copying squares. The children were pretested by being given an 8½ by 11 inch piece of white paper upon which to copy a square. Each week two fewer children were included in the experiment so that after about a month only six children were left, and they had been saturated with nearly daily square-making exercises. They had constructed squares out of paper strips, had cut out predrawn squares, had run their fingers around square pieces of cardboard, had picked square shapes from an assortment of shapes, and had been thoroughly bombarded with tasks to increase their square-copying ability. A posttest was given to all youngsters. It was thought that those children who had had the most experience would have improved the most in their ability. Such was not the case. Some of these children had improved, but some actually made poorer squares on the posttest. There was no relationship between the amount of training the children had received and their ability to copy squares.

When these same children returned the following year as "seniors" in the nursery school, they were again asked to copy a square, to see if the learning that supposedly took place during the square-making exercises would finally come to fruition. A second, untutored group of senior children were also asked to do the same task. Indeed, there had been an amazing improvement over the summer, and all the children could make some semblance of a square. However, the experimental group showed no greater square-making ability than did the children who had not had the opportunity to develop this skill. The training seemed to be of no value.

Possibly the wrong kind of exercise was used to try to teach these children. Maybe physically manipulating forms and tracing around shapes is irrelevant if copying shapes is a cognitive function. That is, the developmental process and a child's awareness of shapes and forms is not limited to lessons with those forms. All children learn how to walk without prescribed exercises such as watching people walk, swinging their legs back and forth, seeing pictures of people walking, or touching somebody's walking legs. Undoubtedly they do many of these things but not for a scheduled 15-minute interval each day. Just as some children walk earlier than others, some children copy geometric shapes earlier than others.

45. A five year old makes spontaneous use of circles and squares to express a human figure. She didn't have to be taught this skill.

Since randomly trying every method one could think of to improve children's square copying ability apparently had not worked, another study was attempted which was more selective. Williams (1970) used three different methods: *a*) a visual method in which children were shown a film portraying a colorful square being made; *b*) a manipulative method which utilized a piece of plywood about three feet square with grooves for removable sides; *c*) a verbal method in which children were shown cards with some shapes on them, accompanied by a verbal description of how each shape was like or not like a square.

One hundred and four nursery school children, boys and girls, three and four years old, were divided equally into four groups, one group for each of the three methods and a control group which merely engaged in nursery school pleasantries for a comparable length of time. All youngsters in the three groups were first asked to copy a square onto a piece of regular typing paper; each was given a comparable sheet, with the square clearly outlined, to use as a model. Each child was tested individually in his own nursery school at a relaxed pace. The pretest of copying a square was followed by three training sessions of five to ten minutes each, within a period of several days. The posttest was also simply copying a square. All copies of the square were put into a pile. Seven judges then independently sorted these, from poorest to best.

Although the degree of improvement was small, a significant number of children in the group that sorted cards with an adult verbalizing about them, and a nonsignificant number of children in the group that manipulated the wood square, improved in square-copying ability. Results were most pronounced for the four year olds. Girls tended to improve most after the verbal method and boys did better after the manipulative task. Because of the unexpected male-female difference, it may be that a combination of these methods would provide a means for developing successful copying abilities. It appears that the interaction between the child and the stimuli is an important consideration in such learning. Since there was a relatively small degree of improvement observed in the copying ability of these children, there seemed to be no jus-

46. *Children will draw straight lines and make intersections in their own drawings before they can copy triangles and diamonds successfully.*

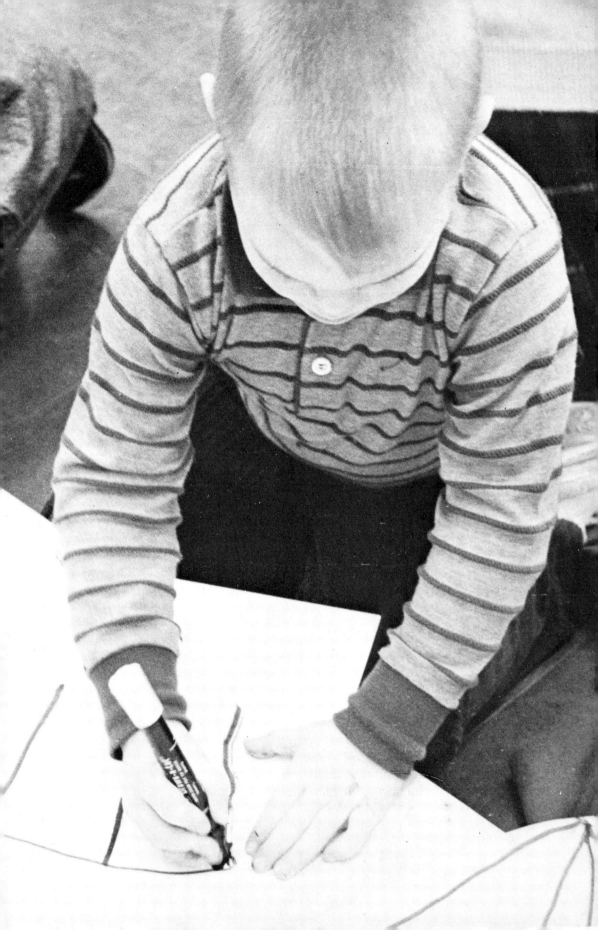

tification for establishing such training activities for preschool children.

It should be emphasized that the investigators in the above studies were not interested in developing methods to improve square-making ability, but were trying to clarify some of the problems and identify the areas that need to be investigated to give us a better understanding of the factors involved in drawing behavior. Certainly the small degree of improvement in square-making ability by the population indicates that it would be far easier to wait a year for three year old children to mature sufficiently to perform such a task than it would be to spend nearly the same length of time in what is basically a frustrating task for both the child and the teacher.

We found no magic age at which certain aspects of copying were most easily learned, such as producing the correct number of angles or making straight lines. One study (Graham, Berman, and Ernhart, 1960) of the ability of 108 preschool children to copy forms concluded that there are no discrete learning stages; instead there is a gradual improvement in ability to make straight lines or intersections. It appears that learning to copy is a slow process without any critical periods, a process that takes much interaction, involvement, and learning about things other than geometric forms.

Copying Familiar Forms

Young children have difficulty copying geometric forms. However, if these forms have meaning for the child, his ability to copy might improve sooner than if he is merely asked to copy a meaningless shape. It was thought that asking a child to copy a familiar shape might be an easier task than having him copy a comparable geometric form. Trisdorfer (1972) tried to find out. A triangle was selected as the stimulus since three to five year olds show varying degrees of ability in reproducing it. The normal age for success in triangle copying is about five years (Gesell, 1940, puts it at five years, three months). The subjects for this

47. *"Can you find the witch's hat? See if you can make one just like it." This task did not seem easier for most children than copying a triangle.*

study were the same 48 preschool children mentioned earlier in this chapter. They ranged in age from three years eight months to five years seven months. The subjects were tested individually; they were first shown a triangle on a separate piece of paper and then asked to "make one just like this on your paper." The second task was to copy a drawing of a witch's hat (a triangle with an accentuated peak and an elongated base), which was shown along with drawings of three other hats, including a top hat, a lady's hat, and a mountain climber's hat. The two sets of triangles, copies of the simple triangle and copies of the witch's hat, numbering some 96 drawings, were judged for accuracy.

There was no significant difference in copying the triangle versus copying the hat. The ability to copy a triangle accurately followed a definite progression with age. Twenty-one of the 48 children scored equally well on their copies of both the triangle and the hat. These copies were examined more carefully, and most of the drawings of the hat indicated either a more clearly recognizable peak or base. Although the children knew they were copying a witch's hat, the triangle was not easier to reproduce even when placed in a more familiar context. Therefore, it appears that it is not easier for a nursery school child to copy a geometric shape just because someone calls it by a more familiar name.

Copying and Shape of Paper

All of the copying examples mentioned in these studies were done on the usual 8½ by 11 inch white paper. In fact, most of the opportunities that children

87

48. *Sometimes a child
paints lines parallel to the
edges of his paper, so
that the resulting picture
has an obvious reference
to the rectangular page.
Such is the case with this
painting by Michelan-
giolo, a young Italian
boy.*

have to draw or mark are on comparable paper. The
norms for copying tasks are established on such
paper, and no one has seemed to question what would
happen if we all used triangular or round sheets of
paper. In copying a square, do young children use the
edge as a reference (as suggested by Brissoni, 1975,
working with children in Italy)? Is this why the
square with four sides and right angles to worry about
can be copied so much earlier than the triangle, which
only has three sides and no parallel lines? Mastering
the triangle with its diagonal lines takes an additional
year beyond the time when a child can usually copy a
square. Interestingly enough, although he cannot draw

one, there is no comparable time lag in a child's ability to identify a triangle in a series of geometric forms. Some rather extensive work has been done on examining the problem of why the diagonal line is difficult for children to make (Olson, 1970).

However, a simpler question was asked in a further study (Brittain, 1976): What is the effect of various-shaped pieces of paper on a child's ability to copy geometric forms? Although it is normal for a four year old to be able to copy a square on a rectangular piece of paper, perhaps the same child would not be able to copy a square on a triangular piece of paper. Three groups of nursery school children ranging in age from three years three months to five years one month were asked to do several copying tasks, two or three times during a month. The tasks were to copy a circle, a square, and a triangle separately on four different-shaped pieces of paper. Each child thus had 12 copying tasks to perform. Only those children who were interested and carried out the complete series were included in the study.

The first group of 13 children tested were from a cooperative nursery school. Since the findings looked rather interesting, another group of 20 children from the Cornell University Nursery School were also asked to do the same copying tasks. And just to be sure, a third group of 20 children from a community nursery school were tested with the same tasks. A teacher-type person worked with each child individually and somewhat removed from each nursery school's activities. The three forms used as a model were each drawn with black ink on standard white 8½ by 11 inch paper. However, the children copied these with felt-tipped pens on paper cut into the shape of a circle, a square, a triangle, and an amorphous somewhat kidney shape, each about 80 square inches. The copying order was random so that no two children copied the forms in the same order. After being given a short time to experiment with the pen, the children were asked to copy the model. "Here is a square. Will you draw it on this paper?" All copies of each geometric form were shuffled together regardless of the background shape and were then rated on a five-point scale, with zero being a scribble and five being an excellent copy.

As could be predicted, when examining all of the copies on all of the various shapes, the circle was the easiest form to copy, with the square next, and the triangle the most difficult. However, there was little difference between scores for copying a circle on circular paper, a square on square paper, and a triangle on triangular paper. In fact, copying a triangle on a triangular paper was as easy as copying a circle on triangular paper. One of the most difficult tasks for these children was to copy a square on a triangular shape.

49. *Keeping children at the task of diligently copying geometric forms didn't produce any better copying than did just waiting for these children to mature.*

Since it was just as easy for the children to copy a triangle on a triangular piece of paper as it was to copy a square on a square piece of paper, some inferences could be made. One could assume that the child who seems to be copying a square may not be doing that at all, but may be merely following the edge of the paper. The most common mistake that children made in copying a square on a triangle was to make it three-sided. Possibly we are not being accurate when we say that a four year old can copy a square. What we may actually be saying is that a four year old can use the paper edge as a reference while drawing in order to produce a square. This indicates that the usual developmental sequence of circle, square, and triangle may be partially a result of using the typical four-sided background paper. Probably new norms should be established for the age when children acquire the ability to copy geometric forms on a background of indefinite shape.

A closer analysis of some of these drawings indicates that those children who obviously used the edge of the paper as a reference may have been fairly close to being able to copy the form anyway. Being able to recognize the triangular paper as similar in shape to the triangle they were to copy meant that these children were aware of the features of a triangle even though they were not yet able to copy this form. However, because they were able to see the relation between the background paper and the model, they used the edge of the paper as a reference. This seems to be an interim step between recognition of a form and ability to duplicate it.

Perhaps, when seeing outline drawings of geometric forms, youngsters do not interpret these lines as the edges of areas, but merely as individual lines that touch at random points. If so, then the shape of the paper can be used as a reference, and therefore the paper shape would play an important role in determining the success of such copying. Probably most adults see the linear representation of a geometric form as a positive shape, readily removable from the paper. However, some children may not have this concept, but see the outline as merely the random placing of lines on a paper. This would make the copying procedures much more complex and difficult.

One of the conclusions that can be drawn from the studies to date is that there is no justification for trying to teach young children how to copy geometric forms. It is probably not because the method of teaching has not been perfected, but because there are other considerations in the learning process that are not yet fully understood. The ability to copy forms is not closely tied to practice, but seems to be the result of a whole range of experiences that make up the child's intellectual or cognitive abilities. Some children can copy a square, for example, long before the age of four; however, some children cannot do this task for another year. Something intervenes. As might be expected, this is closely tied to intellectual development, which means that some children, because of environmental conditions or some hereditary factor, are able to complete tasks at the age of four that other children cannot do until the age of five.

It would be fairly easy to dismiss the subject at this point, but there are some clues that need to be examined further. In the early stages of the study dealing with the influence of the shape of the background paper on children's copying abilities, one of the experimenters came up with some startling information. She said it was possible for her to determine beforehand which children would successfully do certain copying tasks and which children could not. Because it was felt necessary at that time for children to be able to copy a square before one could tell whether the change of background paper would influence the copy, all children were pretested. The investigator also established rapport with the nursery school group as a whole, which is good practice in any research with young children, so that the experiment itself was not influenced by the sudden appearance of a strange person with TEST MATERIALS. Therefore, the investigator spent a week getting to know the children and their behavior patterns, talking with them, watching their activities, and making anecdotal notes.

Those children who could successfully copy geometric forms at an early age had certain characteristics. They were active, curious, and enjoyed looking at books, painting or working with other art materials, and talking to adults as people. Those children who could not do the task successfully were either passive, or enjoyed primarily large-muscle activities such as running or tricycle riding; they did not enjoy reading books and tended to fidget or become impatient when others read to them. They usually had to be encouraged to draw or paint and often did not stay long at that activity, and their interactions with the teacher tended to be largely demanding or avoiding, with very little conversation with or listening to adults.

One way to improve copying ability might be to change the child's concept of what a teacher is, from the idea of a teacher as policeman to that of helper with whom to share experiences. It seems important for the teacher to provide the stimulation and opportunity for the child to draw and paint frequently, and to encourage his self-expression. It is also important

50. Giving a child frequent opportunities to draw and paint allows him to create his own forms. This provides background for his later experiences with specific shapes and forms as he learns to read.

for the teacher to help the child to develop a feeling of pleasure and excitement about books, and to provide the opportunity for children to sharpen their curiosities and to find pleasure in exploring and investigating the unknown. Physical-activity patterns might be somewhat harder to moderate, but the use of small muscles in drawing and painting would be a good start. Possibly the large-muscle activities are a result of a child's trying to avoid disliked activities and to become involved in experiences that are nonthreatening. The encouragement of self-expression, the development of curiosity, the use of drawing and painting are all part of what makes a good nursery school program. Developing copying ability would be an incidental by-product.

The differences between the way a three year old and a four year old can copy geometric forms indicates the tremendous amount of learning and understanding that takes place within one's year's time. Drawing a circle requires a continuous circular movement, with no change in direction once the motion has begun; a circle is therefore physically one of the easiest forms to produce. The most common mistake that young children made in trying to copy squares and triangles was to make a closed form that more closely resembled a circle. Whether asked to draw a circle, square, or triangle, one three year old seemed proud to be able to draw a circle each time; he glanced at each model only once before starting, then drew as if the only distinguishing feature of these forms was their closedness. As we have pointed out, a three year old can easily distinguish a circle from other geometric shapes, but the ability to conceptualize these differences in order to achieve a resemblance to the model is more than a perceptual-motor task; it is a new, difficult mode of thinking. The global nonstructured understanding gives way to a refined thinking that not only appears in the awareness of details (four sides, right angles) and the relationship of these parts, but also in the ability to put these conceptualizations into form.

It is probably this latter achievement that is most remarkable; it coincides with the child's ability to abstract and symbolize other aspects of the environment, for when a child can copy a square, he is also making his first representation. The head-feet drawings, the development of symbols for people, signify a big step beyond the closed forms which have made up the scribbles he drew earlier. The ability to successfully reproduce a square and to make representational drawings indicates important growth in intellectual development.

Use of Materials and Spatial Organization

School Art Projects

While making observations in nursery schools, we had the opportunity to discuss a variety of issues with nursery school teachers. Our purpose was to observe children and record their comments while they worked with art materials, but the attitudes and values of teachers became an important consideration as well. The activities were determined almost entirely by the teacher; what she felt important was reflected in the products of the children.

Although there was some variation in each nursery school, the range of art activities was remarkably the same. It was rather difficult for teachers to explain why they were using certain materials, but it was much easier for them to talk about art in a general

97

way. Many of the art activities were obviously not planned for the children, but for their parents or for some aesthetic reason. This was thought to be good public relations, one way of involving parents in the nursery school. Activities planned for parents' benefit included a variety of things, mostly construction projects that were designed for Mother's Day, Thanksgiving, as a Christmas present, or a weekly take-home project. The youngster usually tried to follow directions so that the paper plate would turn out to be a potholder case like everyone else's.

When projects were undertaken primarily for aesthetic reasons, it was clearly the teacher's aesthetics and not the children's that provided the motivation. Some of the nursery schools we visited were decorated with brightly colored pictures, or drawings and paintings by the youngsters, giving an initial impression of a creative and active nursery school environment. Sometimes a few youngsters were singled out as being particularly artistically inclined, and often their pictures were displayed because they were pretty. Projects included dripping paint on paper, folding a still wet painting in half to squish the colors, pasting brightly colored pieces of precut paper randomly on a sheet of paper, and so forth. There seemed to be an emphasis on the end product and on encouraging children to make their pictures look nice. The observers were not sure that the children understood what "nice" was.

Eye-Hand Coordination

Drawing and painting were not utilized to the extent that we initially expected. In explaining why, some teachers expressed the feeling that children would get frustrated with their poor eye-hand coordination when they drew. According to these teachers, drawings often looked like scribbles or were "poor" attempts at representing the environment, so it was felt that, by providing precut or easily assembled art projects, the children supposedly would be less frustrated. Teachers believed that eye-hand coordination would be developed and encouraged more effectively

51. Not all art projects involve the child. This youngster merely plops colored yarn into a container of starch and then onto paper.

by having children trace around shapes or weave yarn through holes in prepunched cards. It was supposed that manual dexterity could be improved in this way and also that young children would be happier with such art productions than if they drew or painted. Needless to say, the observers questioned these assumptions, even though they understood the rationale. It is interesting to note that Montessori, at the turn of the century, thought that children needed to develop eye-hand coordination before they were allowed to draw or paint.

We hypothesized that poor eye-hand coordination had very little to do with the inability of children to draw recognizable objects, and that children would make the same forms regardless of materials used. It is difficult to separate eye-hand coordination from the

52. Drawing or painting on a flat surface does not change the image from the way it would be drawn at the easel; but the paint does not drip.

rest of development. Initially we decided to see if there was a difference in how children drew on a horizontal surface as compared to a vertical surface; the supposition was that different problems in coordination are faced by a child when he is drawing at a low table than when he is drawing at an easel. The table provides the opportunity for small-muscle control, a chance to flex the wrist and elbow, whereas the easel requires that the child stand and use his shoulder and whole arm movements. The easel also provides a more direct line of sight.

The procedure was simply to ask children to draw or paint "another one." If they had been using crayons at a table, then a fresh piece of paper was put on the easel and the crayons were moved as well, so each child could repeat the picture using the same materials on a vertical surface. And of course if a child had been painting at the easel, we moved everything to a table. In examining about 30 drawings and paintings later, it was possible to guess which one was done last, because less time was spent on the second picture. There was no discernible difference between those art products done at a table and at the easel that could be attributed to coordination. The easel paintings could be picked out, however, because the paints had dripped down the paper.

Drawing, Pasting, and Clay

We designed a study to see what influence different art materials had on children's artwork. It was decided that children would be given precut paper shapes to paste and clay to manipulate, to test the hypothesis that these would result in no greater success in making forms than when children drew the same subject. The making of a man was selected as our topic. Two cut paper projects were designed to see if there would be a significant difference between what the child drew and how he constructed his man. The first project was made from brightly colored construction paper cut into geometric forms such as triangles, elongated rectangles, circles, and other curved forms. The second project consisted of comparable materials, but this time these cut paper forms were clearly body parts, with hands and feet attached to arms and legs and with buttons shown on the piece designated as the body.

Twenty-two children from the age of two years eleven months to five years ten months were tested in their home situation. Each child was first asked to draw a man. The materials were an 8½ by 11 inch sheet of white paper and a black fiber-tipped pen. There seemed to be no hesitancy on the part of these children to do this task, although in some cases the children asked if they could draw their brother or friend instead of a man. The drawings were saved to be compared with the construction projects which followed. Next each child was asked to make a man by using colorful geometric shapes selected from the assortment. Once the parts were assembled to the satisfaction of the child, help was given to make sure they were glued securely on the page. There was no time limit on either of these tasks. The next task was to assemble a man from the precut paper body parts. Again the child chose and assembled the various parts as he wished; when he was satisfied, the pieces of paper were glued down. It might be pointed out in passing that the children seemed to enjoy this activity and demonstrated no frustration except for those children who needed adult assistance with pasting. All of these drawing and pasting projects were saved for later analysis.

About two weeks later the same children were again tested in their homes. By now two of the children were no longer available; one family had moved and another was on vacation. This time the children were again asked to draw a man using a black fiber-tipped pen on an 8½ by 11 sheet of white paper. We felt it important to have the second drawing of a man so as to determine whether the first drawing was accidental. We also wondered if the earlier session of assembling body parts to make a man had been somewhat of a learning experience for these children, so that the second set of drawings would be different. Once this task was accomplished, the last activity was using clay to make a man. Each child was given a

53. *Here an experimenter is asking a child to draw a person and recording the child's comments. This seems to be enjoyable for both child and adult.*

grapefruit-sized piece of clay and told he could make a man any way he wanted. Again this seemed to be an enjoyable activity. Children pounded and stretched the clay and had to be reminded occasionally that they were to make a man. The finished clay forms were transferred to white sheets of paper and saved for later analysis.

All of the drawings, paper constructions, and clay models were assembled and arranged according to the age of the child. The drawings ranged all the way from scribbles to a detailed representation of a fairy princess which looked more like the work of a kindergarten child. The paper constructions followed suit; at one end of the continuum the paper was pasted in random fashion, but older children made a good representation of a person with the pieces of paper. The clay products also followed the same pat-

103

tern; the youngest children made blobs or discon-
nected pieces, but older children made a fairly good
representation. It might be noted that most of the
children tended to use clay two-dimensionally. That is,
the clay was rolled into snakes or patted into forms
that could be used to outline or portray the distinguishing features of a person on a flat surface, instead
of the child's trying to construct a three-dimensional
man. Only three of the children actually attempted a
free-standing model.

It was especially interesting to compare all the
works of a single child. The hypothesis that materials
made little difference in the configuration was supported. It seemed to make no difference whether the
child drew a person, made a person from geometric
shapes of colored paper, assembled predetermined
paper body parts, or made a person out of clay; the
same basic forms emerged. If a child had created little
or no recognizable representation (from an adult point
of view) in his pen drawing, he used the other materials in the same manner.

Assembling the body parts made from construction paper proved to be an easier task; at least these
parts were pasted in somewhat better relationship one
to another than was the case with the construction
paper pieces not clearly identified as body parts. In
most cases the second drawing tended to be in a little
more detail than the first drawing. It should be remembered that the second drawing was done two
weeks later; the child was possibly more mentally
prepared for the tasks since the experimenter and the
project were no longer a novelty.

The products of four children, which have been
selected as examples, are in plate 1, facing page 114.
Since the youngest children tended to do random
scribbling and pasting and the older children did the
task with seemingly little difficulty, it was the middle
range that appeared most interesting, so the examples
are taken from that group. The ages of the children
whose work is shown are three years seven months,
four years, four years ten months, and five years four
months.

The youngest child has a drawing that would be
difficult to call a man. A close look shows that there

are some man-like elements there. Pasting the construction paper seemed to be more a matter of ordering parts than making a person, although the second pasting task, that of assembling the body parts, might be construed as being somehow related to a representation of a man. The second drawing seems less man-like than the first, and the clay product is again a mere assemblage of parts in some sort of order with no resemblance to a person.

Looking at the four year old's examples, one is immediately struck with the cohesiveness of expression in each of the examples shown. A rather elaborate arrangement seems to be repeated in each instance. The second pasting task looks most man-like, but seems less characteristic of the child. The clay project mirrors the style of the drawings.

The child of four years ten months has as his typical representation simply a head and appendages. It is only in the second pasting task that a body part is included. But note that even here the arms extend from the head.

The work of the oldest child, five years four months, exhibits what might be thought of as the most naturalistic man. Again, the particular spacing and organization of the representation, arms straight out and legs straight down, seems to be standard throughout, regardless of the means or material used. Although the works of these four children have been selected for discussion, they are typical of the total sample. It was thought that no further analysis needed to be done to support the hypothesis that the art material was not a crucial factor in how children represent their environment. It is clearly not eye-hand coordination or ease of handling the cut paper that makes the task less frustrating to the child. In fact, it was sometimes the older child who felt more frustrated, if a particular body part were not contained in the materials the child was given.

Although the sample was small, it appears that young children are not disappointed in their own means of representation. It is anticipated that these same children would easily be frustrated if their products were rejected or if the experimenter volunteered to show the child how to do it the "correct way." But

106

of greatest importance is the finding that the choice of material plays very little part in the manner in which children represent a person. Assembling precut parts seemed neither to allow more complete representation nor to provide any significant learning that was carried over to the second drawing session.

Maturing Concepts in "Eating" Drawings

The degree of change noted from the work of the youngest to that of the oldest child in this study is dramatic. However, here we had only an isolated object drawn or constructed, albeit an important one, a man. To examine the changes that take place in a child's representation of space and environment, an extensive study was undertaken. Drawings were collected from over a thousand children from two years old through high school age, and from a variety of school settings. Our present concern is only with those drawings made by the two to six year old children, gathered from preschools, day care centers, and kindergartens. Since the investigators wanted to be sure that the differences shown in these drawings were primarily the results of maturation, we decided to use the same simple materials for everyone and to have all children draw the same subject. A black fiber-tipped pen and an 8½ by 11 inch sheet of white paper served as the drawing equipment. The subject was *eating.*

A common motivation was presented for the teachers to use in talking with the children, to get them interested and involved in the subject. In nursery schools and kindergartens the usual classroom teacher presented the lesson, but the circumstances for each school varied considerably. Sometimes the whole group would be drawing at once; often several children at a drawing table would be involved in the project, or individual children would be encouraged to draw on the topic. The motivation given to the teachers in advance of the drawing test was as follows:

54. *A four year old boy drew this picture of himself eating. This might be called a scribble if we didn't know what he was drawing.*

Do you eat? Of course, everyone eats! How often do you eat? More than once a day? Oh, you eat in the morning, at noontime, in the evening! Do you eat the same thing all the time? Oh, no! Sometimes you need to use forks and spoons. Wouldn't it be funny to try to eat soup with a fork? Sometimes do you just use your fingers? Can you make believe you are eating something right now? Oh, notice how you are bending your arms! Some things we can eat faster than others! Here is a sheet of paper and a pen, we are going to draw ourselves eating."

Although these drawings were fascinating when they were spread out for examination, it was the younger children who tended to have the most spontaneous and attractive drawings. We found this interesting since as children grew older they were able to

55. *Five year old Hugh drew head-feet people around what appears to be a table. Notice that the figures are unrelated to one another.*

56. *The hamburger on the plate almost seems to float near the hand. This six year old's symbol for a person stands rigid, with only a finger touching the plate.*

make representations that were more accurate, but that lacked a quality which might be termed *freshness*. The investigators wondered how much of this was caused by the teaching of art.

Once the drawings were arranged according to the child's age, it was relatively easy to see differences in how children represented this topic. The greatest changes occurred in the drawings by young children, although each age had samples of drawings that might easily be seen as the work of a child either a year younger or a year older. That is, some drawings by four year olds looked as if they could easily have been done by three year olds, and some looked as if they could have been done by five year olds. However, in trying to determine what was typical for each age the investigators looked only at the center of what might be called the normal distribution.

The drawings by the younger children were, as anticipated, scribbles. Two and three year olds made marks all over the page, and there was nothing that the observers could identify as being related to eating. The four year olds began to isolate various parts of their paper into scribbles or circles which had some meaning to the child; at least the observers interpreted the filling of spaces and concentrations in line as having meaning. There were also some head-feet representations, some isolated heads, and even what might be thought of as a table or two. The five year olds were clearly drawing representations of eating. However,

57. *James, also six, worked very hard trying to show himself eating. Again we see no table, and he looks at us rather than at the food.*

110

these drawings were of unrelated aspects of eating; a person would be shown along with food, but rarely would these two elements be joined. There was no overlapping, objects were drawn in isolation, and there was no representation of a total environment.

Even the six year olds tended to draw the objects represented in isolation. Although members of the family would be drawn alongside each other, there was little evidence of overlapping and no representation of a total scene. This age group also used some interesting methods of showing food on a table. None of these attempts utilized any rules of perspective; nor did any drawing portray the eating situation as seen from a single viewpoint. It appeared that the child attempted to show what was important for him in the activity, and there was little concern for an objective portrayal of the particular setting. Even when a table was drawn with the family around it, it was as if the child himself took the position at the table for each member of the family, and each place at the table was shown from a different viewpoint. In other instances, the table would be tipped up to show the food that was on it, and members of the family would be standing at attention as if ready for inspection, facing the artist. Sometimes the food would be tipped up or elevated above the table for easier examination; frequently the sides of a bowl would be left off so that we could see the contents, as if the viewer had X-ray eyes and could see through cups or bowls. These interesting variations were continued in drawings by children of seven, eight, and nine years old, and it was not until the age of ten that these distortions and liberties were beginning to be phased out.

An overall view of these drawings certainly indicates that children are not attempting to make a photographic likeness of a particular event, and that possibly they really do not have a total concept or understanding of an event when they themselves are removed from it. That is, each of these drawings gives an indication of the child's personal involvement with eating and shows the eating utensils and food in relation to himself rather than in relation to a single arbitrary viewpoint removed from the child. These are not impersonal drawings. Alterations, distortions, X-ray drawings, and exaggerations are really not that at all,

but are instead honest attempts at portraying an event as the child understands it.

From Scribbles to Spatial Organization

In looking again at the drawings by two year olds we find they are primarily the results of the motions made for the sake of movement itself. As discussed in Chapter 2, the lines follow the swing of the arm, the manipulation of the tool, and become a record of physical activity. However, some three and many four year olds no longer scribble in that same fashion. The lines now indicate other types of motion. The scribble changes from being the result of motion itself to signifying motion in an object. *Eating fast* takes different kinds of motions than *eating slowly*. To represent eating a hamburger requires a type of line different from that used to show eating soup. Although these scribbles may look little changed to the observer, there is an important difference in that the drawings now begin to represent things external to the child; the transfer from motion itself to the representation of motion means that the line has become symbolic.

Of interest in the *eating* drawings by three year olds is the use of the line to symbolize forms. Adults are used to a line symbolizing the edges of objects, but for young children a line may not have this meaning, particularly when they themselves do the drawing. There is no reason to believe that the mere outline of a form would be an important quality that young children would naturally draw. However, we can see the beginnings of line used as outline when we see the closed forms beginning to take on the meaning *hamburger* or *people*. The closed shape seems to be what is important. It may be that this change from having a line be merely a line to having it mean the edge of a solid shape results from a visual inspection of the drawing itself by the child. The circular motion is one of the first to be accomplished, and the circular form can be seen as a line which closes upon itself, or as the edge of a shape such as a disc. A three-dimensional

58. Another kindergartener has arranged his family around the table. This unusual representation shows each person from a separate point of view.

form such as a ball, or in this case a hamburger,
may result because of the recognition that there
is some resemblance between what is drawn and
the outline of comparable shapes in the environment.
This transition does not take long to happen. We find
that five year olds use a line almost exclusively to represent the edges of shapes. However, even here the
line is still used merely to connect the body to the
hand; although the child is very aware that the arm
does have volume, he is unaware that the line is a
poor representation of that quality. The significance of
this rapid change in the meaning of the line becomes
evident when we realize that in nearly all of the art
work that older children or adults produce, the line
takes on the meaning of a contour or edge of an object; it connotes the boundaries of a solid rather than
being the result of a physical direction or motion.

59. *This first grader
shows us the inside of the
house, with objects on
the table and the family
dog also eating. There is
no overlapping and the
people echo the shape of
the chairs.*

PLATE 1
These are representations
of a man, drawn by four
children of different ages.
Each child has his own
characteristic way of ex-
pressing an idea, regard-
less of whether he is
drawing, assembling cut
paper, or working in
clay.

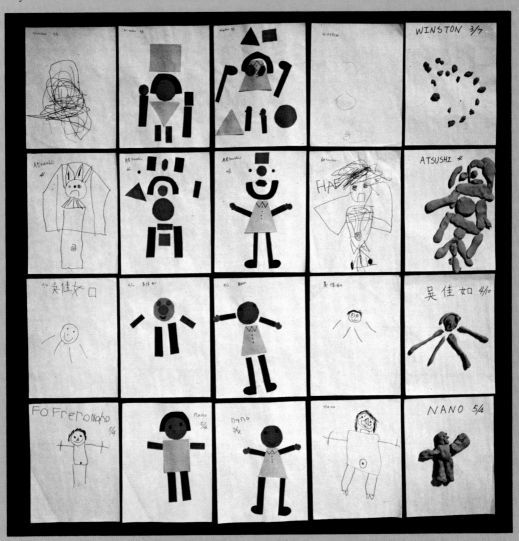

PLATE 2
This painting of faces was made by a young nursery school child, who appears to have enjoyed color with no concern for using it in a naturalistic way.

PLATE 3
Although only blue paint was provided, this did not restrict the child's straightforward expression. His painting fills the paper and was done quickly with no pondering over where to put what form. When it was completed the child, in business-like fashion, removed his smock and turned to other tasks.

Eating seemed to be a subject to which all children could relate. In looking over the drawings it was clear that each child drew from his own experiences. It was his family that was portrayed, it was his table upon which the food was placed, it was his dog that was under the table. This is important to mention since children of junior high school age and older often portrayed this same subject matter in the abstract or drew imaginary persons or settings. Older children would occasionally make up stories about someone else eating in a restaurant, but young children dealt only with their own experiences and did not show any fictitious scenes. Also, in some instances it was a struggle for children to put down what was important to them. The drawings were not easily executed, and some children spent a considerable length of time filling in areas or devising methods to portray the essential elements of eating. This was a difficult assignment, but at the same time it seemed to be a

60. *Notice the light rays and the open top on the glass in this first grader's drawing. However, he is still looking straight ahead.*

challenging one which demanded some problem solving. It was here that the uniqueness of each child became apparent. It was necessary for him to extract from his past experiences those images that were central to the scene; then he had to organize the space on his paper to include these and then portray them in such a way that they would make sense to himself and to a viewer.

The drawings by these young children tend to have an add-on quality. Each object is isolated in space, and it is treated as an entity. That is, the various objects are shown removed from any context, free from environmental influence. There are no shadows, no overlapping, little awareness of relative sizes, and only the barest essentials are portrayed to connote meaning. For example, a table almost invariably has all four legs shown, although these legs may go off in different directions. Since it is difficult to see

61. *By the time a child has completed his preschool years, he has shown great growth in his concepts and in his artistic ability.*

all four legs at the same time without one or more being concealed by the tabletop, such a drawing would be inaccurate. However, children did not worry about any discrepancy between the visual image that they had and the table that they drew. There was no comment like "my table is not right," nor was there any attempt to erase or modify a line because of inaccuracies as adults might interpret these. A table actually does have four legs, and therefore it could be considered that this is a more accurate representation of a table. There were also different methods of showing the tabletop itself. Sometimes the tabletop was drawn as a square, but the legs would still be shown. It may be that the child has an egocentric point of view and drew the table as if viewed successively from each side.

The *eating* drawings provide the investigators with a clearer understanding of the importance of art for preschool children. The changes that take place between two and six years of age are greater than changes that take place at any other period of time. This change, from scribbles to representation and then to an organization of subject matter, within this short period, is amazing. To some extent the rest of the drawings of older children merely show a refinement of the concepts that were developed at this early age and a greater attention to portraying the environment with a more photographic likeness. The whole concept of artistic expression is well established by the age of six.

6

Interpreting Young Children's Drawings

Adult Impressions of Children's Art

Paintings by young children are usually bold, with bright colors; they exhibit a freshness and spontaneity that one does not see in paintings by older children. The drawings are simple and direct; the people represented by four and five year olds are usually drawn with just enough detail to connote meaning, with a large head and customary big smile. Even the scribbles of young children are fascinating, and occasionally adults make guesses as to what the child is trying to portray.

It is this latter point that we examined in some detail. Can adults understand what a child is trying to do when he makes a drawing or a painting that does not have clear subject matter? A scribble was shown

119

62. *This youngster is busy drawing something; just what it is may be open to question, but whatever you guess is probably wrong. Most children will be happy to set you straight.*

to 20 adults and a record was kept of their responses. The question was simply, "What do you suppose this child was trying to draw?" The answers provided a good indication that possibly adults see in children's drawings whatever they themselves are looking for. One person said that a drawing was an attempt at making a hippopotamus, another said it was someone eating, another said it looked like the youngster was drawing his mother, another suggested that this might be a drawing by a disturbed child, and so forth.

Sometimes adults look at drawings and paintings by young children to try to determine the psychological well-being of the child. The forms are scrutinized in the abstract; the placement of the drawing on the page is examined, and often the color is thought to have some esoteric meaning. Children's drawings differ one from another, and there is reason to believe that these differences are not accidental. For young children particularly, if they are not attempting a likeness of a given object, it might seem logical that the colors selected or the forms used could express an inner feeling and reflect the mood of the child at the time of the painting, or perhaps reflect deep-seated reactions to the environment. This overlooks the obvious fact that children also enjoy painting just to see the paint; it ignores the possibility that circles and lines may be the result of the child's attempt to control his drawing tools, and that muddy colors may be the result of painting yellow over black and thus be merely the manifestation of the child's explorations in color mixing. It is ridiculous to arrive at conclusions about a child's mental health by diagnosing drawings or paintings we have not seen him creating.

Influence of Experiences on Drawings

One of the questions we have attempted to answer was whether a child's drawing is in fact influenced by previous experience. Mauer (1971) spent considerable time working with 32 preschool children. He had them draw before and after a variety of expe-

riences, as well as with no special experience, to determine what influence these had on their artwork. Mauer devised both reflective and exciting activities for the children. On the reflective side, he asked them to examine and talk about an earlier drawing of their own; on the exciting end of the list he provided an elaborate jack-in-the-box contraption which children found very stimulating. All of the drawings were judged for a range of variables, including the amount of pressure made with the drawing implement, the

63. *Most nursery school pictures are colorful, with abstract line quality. This child felt it was important to paint his pen drawing with large masses of color.*

122

amount of space utilized, the degree of representation, and so forth. However, these experiences did not seem to influence the drawings of the nursery school children. There was no significant difference between the drawings that were done before the experiences and those that were done after.

Of course, there were other differences: four year old children tended to draw more representational images; three year olds tended to make more scribbles; girls made more attempts at human figures; and middle-class children drew more people than did poor children. The biggest difference between the drawings could be considered developmental. That is, three year olds drew like three year olds, and five year olds drew like five year olds, regardless of the type of stimulation or experience that preceded the drawings.

The fact that children's drawings do not reflect the influence of immediate experiences came as no surprise. Earlier, Thomas (1951) hypothesized that nursery school children would paint at lower developmental levels after they had been frustrated. He had several gaily decorated boxes which were rattled and peered into, but when the child wanted to open the box, it was held out of his reach. Thomas opened a few boxes of toys, but held them himself and did not allow the youngsters to touch them. Instead the child was told to paint a picture. Thomas compared the pictures by the children thus frustrated with those that were painted by the same children earlier and by a matched group of youngsters who were not thus frustrated. He found no significant differences either in color, use of form, or line quality. He did find the usual differences in age levels, but not due to the frustrating experience.

The Meaning of Color

Nursery school art is usually thought of as being abstract but colorful. Color often plays an important part in the selection of drawing and painting materials for these youngsters. Although adults may draw with a black pencil, charcoal, or ink, it has been considered

important that young children have plenty of color. Some of the literature maintains that paintings by children are indicative of their psychological well-being and that preschool children express emotions and feelings through their art. We have already seen that some experiences apparently have no immediate effect on youngsters' drawings. Color, however, is a different element, and some studies have been done which tried to relate color to psychological factors in children's behavior.

Alschuler and Hattwick (1947, 1969) presented a rather complete study which attempted to relate the personalities of nursery school children to their drawings and paintings. They studied the paintings of 150 nursery school children for a year and concluded that the psychological maturity of these children was revealed in their color choice, line-type preference, and use of form. However, their results have not been universally accepted. A study by Corcoran (1954) showed that the order in which colors are placed in the easel tray influences how these colors are used by the children. Three year old children tended to use colors at the easel in sequential order. Corcoran concluded that the use of color is one of direct application rather than of selective discrimination between colors. Biehler (1953) used a grid pattern overlay on youngsters' drawings. He found that nursery school children tended to apply colors in a direct relationship to their position on the easel tray. He also reexamined some of Alschuler and Hattwick's statistics and concluded that they had gone beyond a conservative interpretation of their data. Apparently, then, color in itself may not reveal the inner personality of preschool children; probably children enjoy painting with colors with neither conscious or unconscious deliberation, but enjoy reacting to color as they paint.

For most children in nursery school, form seems much more important than color anyway. As definite shapes evolve, they seem to be painted with whatever color is at hand. People can be painted red or green or blue without concern. Even in the drawing process, using a colored felt-tipped pen, children apparently pay little attention to the colored areas in their representation; the outline of the person is more important than the fact that he has on a blue sweater, or a truck

64. *Often children paint their pictures with whatever color is handy. As can be seen from the paintings in the background, this is apt to be right over the color in the easel tray.*

65. *Children seem attracted to color. Frequently painting in large masses, they interact with the painting, modifying and adding color as they proceed.*

66. *(Below) Kindergarten boys are often fascinated by trucks, and can be remarkably observant and knowledgeable about the details.*

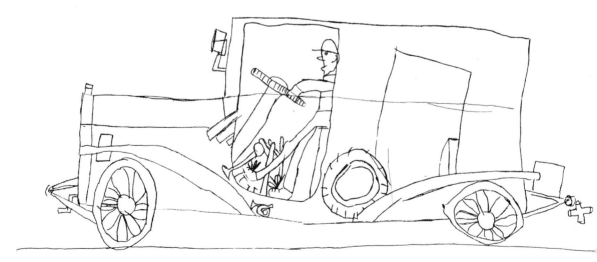

is seen more as a form rather than as a mass of color. Sometimes a five year old will use a red felt pen to outline a truck, and when questioned will tell you that the truck is red. For him, the red outline signifies the color of the object depicted. Some children undoubtedly have a preference for certain colors in their paintings. To say that using red refers to an aggressive tendency, or that painting in black or brown connotes depression, is going a good deal further than the current evidence would suggest.

Art as a Projective Technique

Some adults associate a child's scribble with the mere smearing of paints. This lack of neatness can be seen as a "bad" thing in children and may be why some parents encourage children to use coloring books where the image is predetermined and the child is limited to coloring in a prescribed area. Obviously this limits the use of drawings by these children for diagnostic purposes. But it is questionable anyway whether a child's presumed lack of motor control has any deep psychological meaning.

A survey of the literature on the subject of using art as a projective technique reveals that different clinicians look for different things in drawings; there is no universal symbolism readily apparent in children's drawings. The same drawing by a child can be interpreted in quite different ways by different people, and drawings by children with particular psychotic problems may look surprisingly similar to drawings by normal children. Unless the setting is carefully controlled, with a good deal of information other than drawings available, interpretations of scribbles and early representations by children provide no insight and are of no clinical value to a teacher in a normal school situation.

There is a great risk in trying to interpret children's drawings; there is an even greater risk in trying to deal with children as if this were reliable information. The problem has been pointed out in numerous other studies; our expectations may make us see

67. *At times young
children will show sexual
characteristics in their
drawings, which should
be considered natural.*

something that isn't there. Our behavior toward children may be determined in part by what we think they are saying and doing. Sometimes children's drawings are truthful representations of the world as they know it; this may come as a shock to teachers or parents who read into these drawings other kinds of messages, and who consequently begin to treat the child as if he did in fact have the problems that the adult thought were there. Such an example might be a child who draws a man with an obvious navel and penis. Some adults would be shocked at this display of sexual interest expressed by young children, and might even make comments to the child about such drawings being naughty. However, for the child who is drawing the essential parts of a man, an omission of some of these important parts might be considered just as serious. It could be worse if the teacher saw this particular drawing as an external manifestation of an inner compulsion and constantly watched this child for fear of dire consequences. This may be an extreme example, but anyone who has read the literature on art therapy, of which there is a great deal, can understand that adults might jump to conclusions that have no basis for support in experimental psychology.

Art as a Measure of Intelligence

All of this does not mean that children's drawings cannot provide a valuable clue to child behavior. One of the best documented uses of children's drawings is that they provide an understanding of intellectual development. One widely used measure of intelligence is the Draw-A-Man scale developed by Goodenough and revised by Harris (Harris, 1963). Its main use has been in assessing the intellectual status of young children, particularly those with a language difficulty or hearing handicap. The test is based primarily upon a child's increasing awareness of his environment and the number of details included in the drawing.

Scribbles are not scored on the Draw-A-Man scale. It is only when children begin to draw recognizable objects that scoring can take place. Therefore, the use of drawings as measures of intelligence using this standard scale is not usually of benefit in the nursery school. The whole concept of intelligence is based primarily upon the ability of children to perform in ways that are normal for their chronological age. A child at the age of four who is performing at a level comparable to that of a five year old is therefore a child who is above normal in intellectual development. By the same criteria, a child who is not capable of performing certain tasks which involve developing relationships, or of understanding concepts normal for his age, may be considered below the norm in his intellectual development. The process of drawing can be understood within this framework. Those children who are still making uncontrolled marks on the page, who have not developed the ability to produce closed forms, or who have not developed some relationship between the marks on the page and their environment, may be considered to be at the three year level, where

such drawing is normal. The drawings and paintings by children can then be seen as an important reference and guide for planning meaningful programs for pre-school children.

By kindergarten most children are making draw-ings that can be judged on the Draw-A-Man scale. It is not the score on any scale that is important, but rather the implications or meaning of that score for helping us deal effectively with the child in a learning

68. *A girl of four and a half years has drawn a person. Note that there is a closed form for the head, with eyes and some lines which may stand for arms and legs.*

situation. A child who is still scribbling in kindergarten is not intellectually ready to deal with factual information, to follow directional instructions, or to recognize positional differences in letters, all of which may be required in a reading readiness program designed for five year olds. No amount of scolding, extra work, or remedial help will make the child mature faster. What is needed is an understanding on the part of the teacher that some of the tasks will be frustrating to this youngster; he needs support and success experiences at his own level of competence. Otherwise school can brand him a failure in kindergarten, and he will know it. At some point his scribbles will be replaced by recognizable objects, and the child will be able to deal more effectively with the reading program. There is nothing that says "Thou shalt begin to read at age six." A study of children's reading readiness in three kindergartens (Sibley, 1957) found that

69. *Here a girl of four years and one month also has drawn a person; but notice the great amount of detail which is included, quite unusual for this age.*

drawings gathered from these children gave a better prediction of how well they read a year later in first grade than did the estimates of the kindergarten teachers.

Art as an Outlet for Emotions

When planning programs for young children, it is wise to realize that, for some of them, art provides a catharsis. We have observed children using art activities as a means of expressing themselves in a very open way. Some of these feelings are obviously transitory in nature, with children first making round shapes from clay and then commenting that they hate stones and pounding the round shapes flat. Often one sees a child who is very excited about painting as if he had something important to express, although the content may not always be clear to an observer. Using art in this way has great value. Just the act of painting provides an avenue for release of tension and discharges a good deal of energy. The finished painting itself is evidence of an accomplishment, the creation of a new form which carries with it that which was expressed. In a sense, this is like an adult who writes a nasty letter, only to tear it up later, but who feels better for having gone through the exercise. Young children have as many frustrations as adults, and they may very well not be able to deal with these in as rational a manner. Being able to express emotions in a socially acceptable manner provides a framework for emotional growth.

Often art activities are looked upon as play. Fortunately, teachers of young children understand the importance of play. Although art is usually pleasurable, play often has other connotations; it may be considered frivolous, amusing for the moment but of no lasting value. From watching children engaged in numerous art activities, we would certainly say that these activities are not considered play by the children themselves. There were times when some tasks that might be called art were treated in a playful manner by children. But this playfulness indicated a lack of in-

70. *Drawing is serious business. Most children approach art with earnestness, whether scribbling or making a detailed drawing.*

volvement; in some cases it was an activity which was beyond the understanding of the child himself. But where expressive art was involved, there was no play. Although there are other good reasons for involving children in a variety of art activities, the opportunity for them to put down on paper their feelings and emotions, whether conscious or not, provides one excellent reason for the inclusion of art at the preschool level.

For the most part, children do not understand their own drawings as being art. Children do not hide their feelings, nor are they particularly self-conscious about their art. An interested adult can quite easily question children about certain aspects of a painting if it contains subject matter or symbols they don't understand. A simple example was taken from one observer's notes. The child had made a drawing of a figure with elongated legs. On one leg was a large circle which had been blacked in. The observer remarked to the child, "Hey, you certainly have made a long leg there. And look at that big circle on the leg!" The child hurried to explain that the person being drawn had hurt her knee and this was a great big scab. "See, just like me!" Thereupon the child pulled up her jeans to show the scraped knee. One does not need psychoanalytic training to discover that children put into their drawings and paintings that which they have experienced and which is important to them. But a knee is a knee and not a symbol for something else.

Prehistoric Art and Children's Art

The artwork of a single child, collected over a long period of time, will show increasing ability to depict developing concepts and increasing mastery over materials. As he seeks to put order into his world, with his artwork providing the visible record, he moves from crude scribbling to realistic, skillful representations. Harlan (1970) and others have imagined a parallel in development between children and societies, from primitive to sophisticated. A few art educators (Kellogg, 1969) have gone so far as to claim that children's art is like the art of our Stone Age cave-dwelling ancestors, and that it moves through successive cultural stages as the children develop. For a time in the late nineteenth century, this was a popular notion among some archaeologists and anthropologists, but now most scholars have discredited the idea as simplistic.

The human remains found in association with cave art indicate that the artists themselves were little different from modern man. They buried their dead with flowers, cared for their aging relatives, and had a cranial capacity equal to if not greater than our own. Some remains of the beginnings of art, 35,000 to 40,000 years old, are to be found in the caves of northern Spain and southern France. Among the most famous are Altamira, Lascaux, Niaux, Rouffignac, and Pech-Merle. The quality is high and shows mastery of the materials, including black, red, and yellow paints made from ground oxides, as well as carved bone and stone. The predominant subject matter of this Paleolithic art is animals, represented with marvelous accuracy and sympathy (Chancellor, 1964).

Excavation of cave floors revealed paintings on the walls which had been covered by the accumulation of rock, dirt, and debris on the floor. Dating of small articles is simplified when they are discovered in the rubble in an occupation layer separated from other layers by sterile strata (Childe, 1962). Carbon-14 dating has been helpful. Relative chronology of various industries and cultures can sometimes be accurately established; some cultures undoubtedly coexisted. Precise dating is impossible (Torbrügge, 1968). Recent extensive examinations by Marshack (1975), aided by ultraviolet and infrared photography as well as microscope, make it possible to determine the order in which separate layers of paintings were made on a single cave wall. A few theorists believe that there was a steady progression from simple outline drawing to more stylized drawing, and then back to strong emphasis on the outline (Kuhn, 1967). Different artistic styles prevailed at different locations and at different times. There is no uniformity in Paleolithic art; instead, there is great diversity in the artistic conventions and techniques, with a complex interplay of

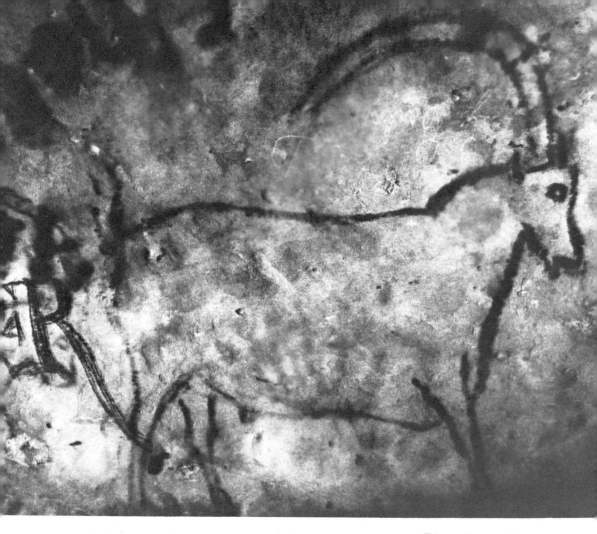

traditions and sharp cultural breaks between them (Ucko and Rosenfeld, 1967).

The simplest works which survive today are not necessarily the oldest. The first artistic attempts were probably made on perishable organic materials. Works complex in concept and technique are among the oldest surviving. During 20,000 years or more of the Paleolithic period, experimentation and discovery as well as contacts with other cultures influenced the art works. Ucko and Rosenfeld point out that in art, as in any other field of study, development is often interrupted by stagnant periods, standardization, and

71. (Above) This goat was painted thousands of years ago by Paleolithic man in a cavern at Rouffignac, France. Modern man has added some graffiti.

136

even regression. There are many beginnings, many climaxes. Conquering the technical difficulties in producing some of the carved works may represent a far greater achievement than painting a picture which we find aesthetically pleasing.

Scholars believe that the paintings often depict not just any bison or mammoth but a particular animal. These people had a hunting culture, requiring a cooperative society. According to some scholars (Taralon, 1962), representing an animal faithfully may have had a magic intent; perhaps making an image of the quarry would enable the hunter to control and dominate the animal he hoped to kill. In some cases wounded animals are painted. Some carvings show the evidence of much wear and handling, as if they had been kept and used for a long time (Marshack, 1975). Most of these magnificent animals seem very alive and are depicted with sophistication showing that the Paleolithic artist was far from childlike. He was able

72. *This is an unusually detailed cow, drawn by a kindergarten child. There is a great deal of difference between this cow and the goat.*

to give the impression of movement and to use perspective. He took advantage of irregularities in the wall surface to help in his representation, leaving flat walls blank. He drew and painted from memory, by a flickering light, in the deep recesses of the caves. Certainly his art ability is admired by many a modern artist.

Marshack suggests that we should also respect the thinking ability of these ancient artists. Engraved markings on a bone over 30,000 years old have been interpreted as complex notations of the waxing and waning moon, depicting the passage of two and one fourth lunar months and recording the passing seasons. This changes the stereotyped image of Stone Age man from a primitive toolmaker and hunter, to a more modern person who kept deliberate and detailed records with complex systems of symbols.

But where, then, are the drawings by the children of these ancient societies? Unless man has changed more than most scholars would like to admit, Paleolithic children must have been drawing in the sand or playing with clay, scribbling with charcoal on the shelter walls or on wood, much as we would expect modern children to do. Although there are small as well as large footprints in the clay in some caves, and a few small as well as large handprints painted on some cave walls, there are no clues to the art of these prehistoric children. Trips to many of the Stone Age caves and museums turned up no evidence of child art. Furthermore, these painted caves were seldom lived in, but are in inaccessible places. If they were ceremonial places for religious observance, children would probably have been excluded. According to Waage (1967), ". . . the Palaeolithics were not children making pictures in kindergarten; they were adults trying to stay alive in the world." In looking over the evidence we have gathered, there seems to be little reason to continue the myth that children's art parallels early man's graphic development.

7

Role of the Teacher

Importance of the Teacher

Although it is possible to discuss children's learning in abstract terms, and to note that there are stages of development in art, the motivational and environmental forces that make it possible for learning to take place are the responsibility of an adult. What the adult does, how he or she reacts to the child, makes a tremendous difference in how the child views himself and his environment. We are talking about more than just social interaction. Learning is an *active* experience in which a child must react to things around him, assimilating information and adjusting his behavior; he basically must want to explore, find out about, or resolve these experiences into a meaningful context, or learning cannot take place. The teacher, therefore,

139

needs to provide the motivation and psychological environment which makes this possible.

The teacher may not be as important for older children as for young children. Older children can turn to the subject matter itself for information; an interested student can read, ask questions outside of class, discuss issues or seek answers to questions with peers, or visit the library for additional information. Few of these things are available to the nursery school or kindergarten child. The preschool teacher, therefore, becomes most important; the teacher is the one

73. The preschool environment must not only provide the physical setting and tools for learning, but must also provide psychological support.

74. *An interested adult increases children's involvement in art. If adults see these activities as important, children do, too.*

who determines the activities, gives support for action, hands out praise and criticism, and decides the length of time to be spent on whatever projects may be planned. Art activities are particularly vulnerable to the expertise of the teacher.

Influence of Teacher Behavior

During our observations of the art activities in nursery schools and kindergartens we of course also observed the adults who were working with these children. We found many excellent programs in which the teacher was considered outstanding. Most of the adults worked hard trying to keep control of all the

141

variables within the classroom. We were impressed with the dedication of these teachers. But, in spite of our appreciation of the difficulty of the teacher's role, we were able to see outstanding teachers as well as some who made us wonder why they were in the profession. After gathering drawings by the children, our discussion sometimes strayed to a comparison of teaching methods, and this invariably led to a consideration of the personalities of the teachers themselves. What makes a good teacher in the early childhood area? Although there seemed to be common agreement that certain teachers were considered good, it was often difficult to describe why we thought so.

We turned to some of the earlier studies we had made in the Cornell Nursery School for clues. When we were looking at scribbles for meaning, we had draped a microphone over the easel in the nursery school. In listening to the tapes that resulted from the painting sessions, it was quite clear that children communicated very little verbally with an easel. However, when these same children were asked to draw and paint with an adult present who was keeping a record of their drawing motions, the children were quite verbal and freely explained what was going on in the drawing process. What is of interest here is not the fact that children can talk to teachers more easily than they can to an easel, but that the length of time the children spent drawing and painting with an adult present was nearly twice as long as when no adult was present. It also appeared that the adult was not there to direct the drawing or give instructions, but rather to serve as a sounding board, so that an interest in the drawing expressed by only an occasional grunt or an "I see" was sufficient to encourage further drawing and verbalization.

In our study of the videotapes taken of children drawing and painting (Brittain, 1970), it was noted that the teacher could be either a positive or a negative influence on the creative process. One tape showed the children working with clay. Two children were obviously very engrossed in the work and were busily rolling, punching, and manipulating the clay. Forms soon appeared that might be called thumb bowls. The children recognized these as teacups and proceeded to "drink" from these with much animated

75. *This girl has mastered the paper punch. The purpose for punching holes has been forgotten, but notice the achievement.*

conversation. At this point, when the teacher remarked that the children should keep the clay away from their mouths, the two youngsters put down their cups, and went off into other activities.

In another example, a four year old girl was trying to make a paper punch work. She was obviously having great difficulty, but apparently the paper needed to be punched for the project which seemed to be some kind of pasting exercise. Although the teacher appeared in the background, there was no verbal interaction, and the child continued stubbornly to tackle the problem. Luckily, the TV camera was so located that the child remained in view for about ten minutes. The paper buckled and tore and the child temporarily lost interest and gazed around but soon came back to the task at hand. The fingers were placed in the punch handles in different ways, and a two-handed approach

76. *Sometimes the best thing a teacher can do to help children in their art activities is to give no advice or directions at all, merely being nearby and interested.*

was tried. All at once it worked, and this was repeated again and again. Not only was this procedure successful, but the child had such an elating experience that the paper was completely mutilated and the original pasting task was forgotten in the success of making holes. In this instance the teacher did not intervene and do the punching for the child.

One other example showed the nursery school teacher actively involved in helping children in the woodworking process. Some children were sawing, some were hammering, and all of them were having difficulty. However, the teacher was pointing out that the wood needed to be held in the vise if it was to be sawed, that the hammer needed to be held further back on the handle to make it easier to drive the nail, that one piece of wood had to be firmly held if they were to be successfully joined, and at the same time the teacher was constantly giving support and encouragement. The girls were enjoying this experience as much as the boys were.

From listening to and watching these tapes we concluded that there is no set formula for what to say to children. Sometimes it is better to let a child struggle on his own to master a problem; it is usually good to listen to children and to offer suggestions when they seem frustrated or bored. It was thought that constant praise was not good, particularly when indiscriminately administered, but it looked as if constant direction was not conducive to getting children involved either. It was recalled that an earlier study (Lippitt and White, 1960) tried to find out what effects adult leaders had upon 11 year old children. These adult leaders behaved in ways that might be called authoritarian, democratic, and laissez-faire. Among other things, they found that these 11 year old children exhibited a great outburst of horseplay when they were released from the authoritarian leader, and that the children under the democratic leader showed the greatest amount of individual differences and were at the same time less irritable and aggressive toward fellow members.

Because this study had been done with older children, it was thought possible that different findings would come from using the same procedures with nursery school children. Consequently, as part of a class project in early childhood education, students were asked to work with children and follow methods that were authoritarian, democratic, or laissez-faire. These student teachers were responsible for the art activities of nursery school children. It was anticipated that children would draw and paint longer under the direction of the democratic teacher, less under the laissez-faire teacher, and would tire of the activity quickly under the authoritarian teacher. However, the results were surprising. Each student-teacher assumed the three different roles at different times. The greatest length of time that children spent was, as predicted, with the teacher who performed in a democratic way, one who gave guiding suggestions, asked for the children's opinions, and assumed a democratic attitude. However, the laissez-faire teacher, who did not take an active part in giving directions but merely provided materials, was the teacher who had the shortest interest span from the nursery school children. The authoritarian teacher, who issued orders and directions and gave criticisms, was the one who held children's interest for an intermediate length of time. Apparently, it was more important to talk to children, regardless of what was said, than to be indifferent toward them.

Approaches to Creative Activities

Frequently the art activities were given over to teacher aides. At times parents would help or a student from a nearby educational institution would be responsible. Sometimes the art activities were a part of a larger unit that happened to be underway at the time, or were used to demonstrate some sort of skill or knowledge that the child was supposed to learn or assimilate. Under these conditions it was not surprising that we observed many methods of working with children in the arts.

It was fairly common for teacher aides and even head teachers to play the role of housekeeper. They would often spend considerable time in the preparation of materials. This meant getting to the location before the children, mixing up powdered paint, fixing

PLATE 4
This boy is old enough to be able to write his name, but his painting is more exploration of the paints than self-expression. It is important to find out what paints do and how colors merge, and to gain control of the brush.

PLATE 5
Kindergarten children are interested in the world around them. This crayon drawing of a mother bird feeding her young was done by an observant girl. How sad to think that soon she will be asked to color four outlined birds green and two red.

PLATE 6
In this crayon drawing by a kindergarten girl, the clothing was added after the body was drawn. When she colored the skirt, the upper legs became stripes. Criticism, pointing out that the two dots for the eyes are not strong enough or that the legs are not the same width, would not be understood.

the flour and salt combination for playdough, boiling up a mixture of cornstarch and coloring to make finger paint, and so forth. Once the material itself was prepared, the next step was to put it out so that the children could work with it. This meant getting out paper and brushes, or boards for the playdough, clearing off areas to fingerpaint, getting inked pads or string or chalk, cutting up pieces of paper, and so forth. Once the children arrived, it was customary to make a comment, "Wouldn't you like to paint?" The teacher, or teacher aide, or cooperating parent would then make sure there was plenty of paper, get more

77. Organizing art activities takes some thought so that the teacher doesn't end up being merely a house-keeper.

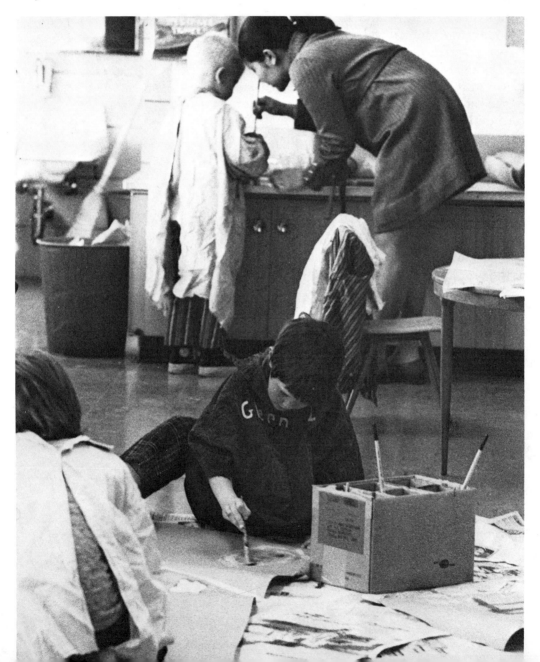

paint, clean the paint off the floor, help somebody
into or out of a smock, direct the children to the
bathroom to wash their hands, or hurry up the
stragglers because storytime was starting. Once the
children left, the adult cleaned up the mess, put away
the supplies, stored the paintings on racks or hung
them on clotheslines, washed off the tables, and then
sat down exhausted.

Because of all the hustle and bustle of the art activity, the adult rarely saw what the child was doing
and rarely made any comments except "Isn't that
nice." Too often the children were left to their own
devices to use the material as they wished, producing
results that were little more than uninvolved dabbling.
A good part of the difficulty seemed to stem from the
use of materials that needed special preparation and
care by the teacher. There was also the implied feeling
that something different must be presented each day
or the children would be bored. It was as if the
teachers thought the children were saying, "What new
and exciting material do we have to play with today?"
But, from the observers' point of view, it seemed that
the constant change of materials in some of the nursery schools actually created boredom.

Even when not busy handing out materials or
cleaning up after children, some teachers were reluctant to talk to children while they were engaged in
art. They felt that somehow the adult was an intruder
in the process. This feeling was expressed in the often-
heard dictum, "Don't ask what it is." It was as if the
creative spirit somehow touched the child from above,
and adults as mere mortals were not allowed to inter-
fere or get in the way of the creative spirit. This
"stand back and watch them create" attitude was
fairly common. We wondered if, because they lacked
formal training in art, these teachers felt unqualified
to explore the possibilities that creative activity offers.
The general attitude toward art seemed to be that this
is an activity that children should enjoy and enter into
freely, but should not be pushed or even encouraged
too much to participate in. Some of the teachers we
spoke to also seemed to feel that if a child does not
paint or draw, he will find some other means of expression. With the prevalence of this sort of attitude,
it was somewhat unexpected that most children did

78. *The teacher of young children must be sensitive to children's ideas and aesthetic taste, and help them with their efforts.*

participate in art activities. It might be pointed out that this idea of children finding their own means of expression may not be so. Some studies indicate (Jones, 1964) that children who expressed themselves easily in one area of the arts are the same children who expressed themselves easily in other areas. Similarly, those children who were hesitant or withdrawn in drawing or painting found it difficult to express themselves in words.

We did note that some of the same teachers who

149

were reluctant to go beyond asking whether their charges might like to paint insisted that the children's hands should be clean after the art experiences, that they had to put on a jacket if they went outside, that shouting could not be tolerated in the nursery school environment, and even that children must sit quietly during storytime. Creative activities were not placed in the same learning categories as other more socially mandated skills. This does not necessarily indicate that these teachers value the arts less, but rather that they are not sure of the proper procedure to encourage participation, and therefore it may seem to them safer to do nothing.

We also observed the opposite extreme in a few kindergarten classes and in three nursery school programs which were cognitively oriented. Here art was treated as just another skill area. The teachers felt that certain skills must be taught before children express themselves, and in some cases the "express themselves" time never arrived. Children were drilled on color names; sometimes paint was withheld until the child could guess the proper name for the color. Demonstrations were given on how to use brushes and how to carefully wipe off the excess paint. A good deal of time was spent in showing children how to draw geometric shapes, or paper was precut in circles, squares, or triangles so that children could properly identify these as they pasted them one over the other to make stereotypes of houses or whatever. We even saw duplicated sheets of outline drawings handed to the children; they were supposed to color in the appropriate colors, making flowers yellow and leaves red and green. All of this was included as art activity.

The basic assumption in such a program is that the teacher knows how children learn, and that it is possible to separate the various elements of the task into palatable segments disguised as art activities to be fed to children. From our observations, we doubt that many teachers really understand how children learn, and certainly the available evidence gives no support for supposing that the teacher who spends considerable time teaching factual material has any success in achieving the desired goals. Our own experience in trying to teach children how to copy squares, as mentioned previously, indicates that some of these activities can be frustrating for both teacher and child. The child doesn't understand what is expected, and the teacher doesn't understand why the child doesn't learn.

Instructional Environment

Because our observations of children engaged in art activities took place in several locations, it was interesting to note the ecological changes that took place as we observed older children. The first thing that impressed us was the fact that environmental conditions varied considerably and in some cases were far from ideal. Most nursery schools were not located in public school buildings, but in church basements, community buildings, or even an abandoned army warehouse. This may have accounted for part of the informality that seemed to exist in environmental arrangements. Rooms for nursery school activities would often have several alcoves, adjoining rooms, or storage areas that would break up the larger space into areas that could be utilized for a variety of activities. Usually art was limited to one particular area. Other areas were given such names as large-muscle room, quiet room, story room, block activity room, and so forth. These rooms or areas were frequently painted different colors, and for the most part children seemed to feel free to move from one room to another, although certain activities seemed to be encouraged at certain times of the day by nursery school teachers.

In contrast the kindergarten seemed to fare somewhat better as far as physical conditions were concerned. Most kindergarten rooms were large, rectangular in shape, and various activities were limited to designated places near the periphery of the room itself, which allowed the center to be open for movement or dance experiences. In smaller schoolrooms the center was occupied by tables at which children sat for group work. For the most part, kindergarten rooms seemed to be more sterile, and had chairs and desks which appeared to be designed primarily for ease of cleaning. All of the activities could be supervised by one person anywhere in the room.

Both in the nursery schools and in the kindergartens we viewed, the rooms had been carefully arranged by adults. At appropriate cleanup times, the children would put the blocks back in a prescribed manner, put the pans and dishes back in the play kitchen, or rearrange the pillows on the floor in what seemed to be their customary location. Although the nursery school teachers and helpers did not expect that children could do these tasks alone, many kin-

79. *Four or five children work well at one table. Several different art activities may be pursued at the same time.*

dergarten teachers kept children in from recess or kept the class waiting while some children put things back into prescribed places before the group as a whole would be read a story, marched to the gym, or allowed to board the buses.

This change from informality to formality in the learning structure was reflected in the art activities that were considered important for children. It was much more usual in the nursery school setting, particularly when three year olds were included, to gear art activities to small groups of children and to have several different projects going on at the same time. This meant that children not only had a choice of activities but also were able to work in small groups of from three to seven children. Sometimes an adult would supervise a table of nursery school children doing some pasting project; at other times the art activity would require no adult supervision.

On the other hand, a few cognitively-oriented nursery schools and most kindergartens seemed to have art activities designed for the whole group. Those involved learning particular skills such as folding a piece of red paper and proper cutting procedures so that a heart emerged in time for Valentine's Day. A few kindergarten teachers did have art projects scheduled in such a way that children had a choice of painting, drawing, or possibly working with blocks. However, even here there was great concern for conforming to a set schedule. Cleaning up and putting away materials needed to be done within a prescribed time span so that the group as a whole could start on the next activity on the agenda.

It has taken a number of decades to break away from the usual pattern of having the teacher's desk at the front of the room and the children's tables or desks lined up in neat rows, one behind the other. The nursery school does not have this heritage, so there is usually greater flexibility of arrangement and more informal furniture groupings. An interesting question to pursue would be to see if a rigid symmetrical arrangement of space and furniture corresponds to a comparable rigid structure in the teaching program. Undoubtedly the teacher's personality enters into this question, but it is expected that changing one might mean changing the other.

Looking over the products made by children in a variety of settings, we discussed the value of exploring several questions linked to the developmental aspects of the arts. Most of these were rather global in nature, such as "Would children be more creative after prolonged experiences in drawing and painting?" or "Do those children who enjoy drawing develop the manipulative skills to make lettering and writing an easier task?" Although these questions were obviously too broad for us to answer in a limited time, we also wondered if it might be conversely possible to develop an art program which would make children less creative, fearful of their own expression, and more dependent upon someone else for direction.

Basically the question was: Can we devise an art program that would negate all of the things the arts stand for? At first the idea seemed tangential to our interests, but the applicability of our discussion suddenly became apparent. It was decided that the first thing to be done in such a program would be to have all art materials moved to a safe place, just out of children's reach. No child would be able to draw or paint except within the prescribed time set by the teacher. Every lesson would be demonstrated before the children started so that there would be no opportunity for spontaneity or imaginative thinking. Each activity would have a definite end product which would be made by the teacher in advance so that each child could see what he was supposed to do. In this way every child would fail, because none could live up to the teacher's model; some children would fail more than others. Skills would be taught to the group as a whole, with all children following a step-by-step procedure for folding the paper, cutting in the right location, putting the paste in the right place, and so forth. Conformity would be ensured by making all children display their products in unison as they progressed. There would be weekly, or perhaps even daily, coloring activities for which the teacher would trace an outline the night before and run off on a ditto machine for children to use so they could learn to stay between the lines. Rewards would be given for neat-

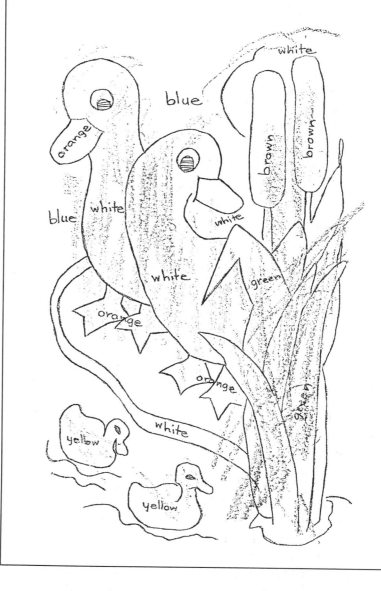

80. *Meaningless stereo-types of almost anything are duplicated for children to color. We found a few of these used in some kindergartens.*

ness and orderliness. Only those products that met the teacher's standards would be praised, and those children who had difficulty in cutting or who somehow were not well enough coordinated so that they could stay between the lines would be given additional exercises in cutting and coloring in order to reinforce their failures. Prescribed stereotypes for any and every holiday would be fed to these children through the dittoed sheets so they would have no opportunity to develop their own relationship to activities outside of school. Pumpkins, turkeys, Pilgrims with blunderbusses, Easter bunnies, and Christmas trees would be issued for children to color under the guise of mathematics or reading, or as a substitute activity for recess when it rained. It was thought that this program would be fairly effective in eliminating genuine spontaneity and creativity from the kindergarten. It would also develop an unquestioning obedience to authority and encourage the learning of meaningless symbols.

Having gone through the frightening exercise of designing a kindergarten art curriculum which would effectively destroy the creative urge within children, it became very apparent that one or two of the teachers in our sample seemed to be striving to do just that. It was anticipated that the teachers in some cases were unconscious of subduing the spontaneity and curiosity of their charges. At times, however, they tried to make blind obedience second nature. One of our observers made a detailed account of a teacher's action in drilling kindergarten children in the proper procedures for a fire drill. Although it is easy to understand the teacher's desire to protect the children in her care, it is difficult to see why she didn't explain the problem and then involve the children in developing procedures. With a quick statement that when the gong sounds all children must jump from their chairs and run against the wall, she proceeded to shout and push and ignore children's questions until they were all standing at attention; then they turned and marched out the door in line, silent, subdued, with really no understanding of what was happening. Pretty much the same procedure was followed during opening ceremonies when children stood and faced the flag and mumbled some incomprehensible words because this was how it was done. Passing from one room to another was treated in the same manner, with quiet, orderly children who knew they must not question why all of this was important. Maybe they learned it was safest not to question anything. There are certain areas of our society where a high value is put on blind obedience and conformity: the military, the penal system, and in some corporations that mass-produce products. There is no evidence that stultifying curiosity, creativity, and imaginative thinking benefits children. The arts, particularly the visual arts, provide an excellent opportunity for the encouragement of spontaneity, originality, and self-expression. From our observational notes, it is apparent that these qualities are not valued very

81. *Finding out how a brush works, manipulating paint into various areas, comparing colors and watching how they merge, these are learnings that cannot easily be programmed.*

156

highly by some kindergarten teachers and that the area of art may be sadly misused.

We may be a little harsh here, since we realize the pressure that most teachers of young children feel. There are a multitude of things to do, many having nothing to do with teaching: taking attendance, collecting milk money, calling parents, ordering supplies, taking care of a sick child, keeping the noise level low, arranging for trips, and so on. But the most crucial factor in any art experience is the teacher, a teacher with sensitivity to the needs of children, one who is aware that children have fears, hopes, and joys that are the bases for art expression.

At one point we had the notion that creative teachers would have creative children in their classes. This was based upon the idea that a teacher is a model and that children emulate certain kinds of behavior. Our notes, however, indicate that this may not always be so. We alluded earlier to a certain creative teacher; we found that this particular classroom of nursery school children seemed to exhibit no more creative behavior, no more imaginative thinking, no more unusual or spontaneous activity than other classrooms. However, other teachers considered this particular teacher to be creative and able to design and plan so many wonderful creative activities for the children in her room. It may be that this was the crucial element; the teacher did the planning and came up with the ideas which the children in the classroom merely executed. The creative thinking was done by the teacher; the children were being told how wonderful and creative they were when they had merely followed directions and sprinkled the sand on the glue or pasted the cottonball tail on the Easter bunny. Such a teacher imposed her ideas on the children just as much as did the teacher who handed out dittoed sheets with outlines to be colored in.

Teaching Recommendations

After spending a great deal of time watching nursery school children paint, we concluded that there is no need for any formal teaching of the procedures of painting to any nursery school child. If there is a learning that takes place, it is not related to the mechanics of art. That is, no child acted as if he were inhibited from lack of instruction on how to hold the brush, how to mix the paint, or how to plan or execute the painting. Instead, every child who painted, regardless of previous painting experiences, seemed to

82. *Jennifer is intently watching the sawing. All learning does not come from the teacher.*

approach the paints, brushes, and paper without hesitation. Admittedly, some children stuck the green brush into the red paint, or experimented with smearing a hand over the painted surface, or painted one color over another until the surface looked muddy, but these deviations from the adult norms certainly did not call for a lesson in painting procedures. The pasting projects seemed to be self-evident to the children, and the three-dimensional materials such as clay or playdough were handled without the need for instruction. They even quickly picked up procedures when working on the woodbench with a variety of tools, some of this through observing others and some through experimentation.

The instructions seemed to be more important when the teacher had a particular goal in mind, such

159

as a marshmallow and feather turkey for Thanksgiving or an orange pumpkin face for Halloween. The youngsters, however, seemed to be involved in an inverse relationship to the amount of instruction received; the more instruction, the less the child was involved. At first this seemed like a contradiction to our earlier findings that a teacher needed to be a part of the activity and to talk to children during the creative process. The difference seemed to be that when the teacher-child interaction was involved with directions so that the project would come out in a particular way, the child's role was primarily that of obeying these instructions or failing. Our earlier experiment had the teacher intervene during the process itself, asking questions, commenting upon the characteristics of the paint, talking to the child about the content of his picture, or even being critical about the amount of paper left unused. It seemed that not only was the amount of interaction between the child and teacher important, but also the nature of this interaction. When the child helped determine the project itself, when his interest and goals were part of the activity, there seemed to be little need for guidance or instruction on the part of the teacher. The greatest degree of involvement on the part of the children took place when the teacher played the role of an interested adult, one who gave support and intervened only when the child seemed hesitant about either his own powers or the next direction to take in the project. This intervention seemed to be more a listing of alternatives for the child to take, such as "How about the rest of your picture?" "Would you rather use a smaller brush?" "Would it be better to wait until that part dried?" or "What do you think you will do next?" This type of interaction was clearly geared toward the purposes and direction of the child himself, and was not of the evaluative or command type which often turned children away from participation. There was no doubt in our minds that the teacher played an important but subtle role in art activities and became the crucial element in making art meaningful to young children.

Children need adult support to be creative, spontaneous thinkers to face and deal with problems at their own level of competence. There appears to be no

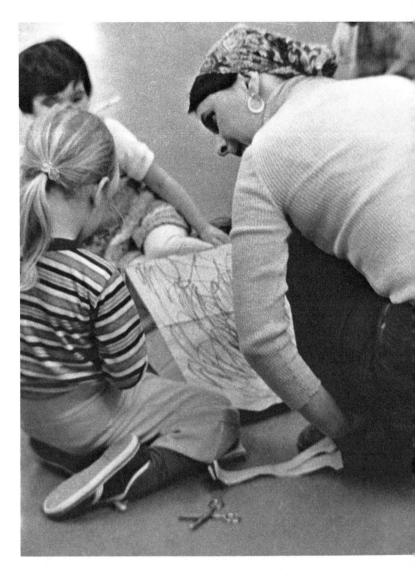

83. *Children appreciate having an interested teacher talk with them about their creative efforts. It is not necessary to give praise.*

reason to try to change a child's mode of thinking. Playfulness, freedom to structure one's own activities, openness to experience, curiosity, are all part of a young child's approach to learning. Because these qualities are not easily maintained without support, they should be on an equal basis with those other areas of learning which stress conformity and compliance to others' thinking.

The teacher often tells the children what to do, even in situations where the problem may be of the child's own making. We are suggesting that not only should the teacher help the child find solutions to problems which are of his own making, and provide possible alternatives for action, but the teacher should also develop problems for the child to solve. "Oh, my, the clay is too hard, what should we do?" "All the brushes are dirty, I guess we can't paint."

Opportunities for children to act upon their environment with their present state of knowledge, even if their actions are neither efficient nor completely understood by the adult, are a critical step in the educative process. The opportunity to explore and investigate the unknown, or to manipulate or alter the known, provides support for children's efforts to think independently. They need to take chances, to question why, to see alternative avenues for action.

One of the ways to provide for greater alternatives for the child is to expand his frame of reference. What is he doing now, how can this be modified, altered, or restructured in ways that can be understood by the child? A teacher who asks for alternatives, such as "What else will you do? Are you going to change it? Where will you put it? Would any other color do?" is providing the child the opportunity to see other directions for his actions—which he can accept or reject. "The clay is over there, the crayons are on the table and the paint is mixed ready to use, which one would you like?" "The easel is a good place to paint, so is the table or the floor; where will you paint?"

There is the unanswered question of what specifically makes a good teacher of the arts for young children. Although they are sometimes treated that way, children don't see themselves as small, cute, or unlearned. If one could play the role of a child for a day, some insights might be gathered about how to teach. Keeping track of the time children spend on the variety of activities, listening to their comments, seeing how much self-involvement takes place, all can contribute to a teacher's understanding of the meaning of art.

Aesthetics and Perception

Aesthetic Behavior of Children

Adults are attracted by the free, spontaneous, and colorful paintings by nursery school children. While working on these studies, we ourselves enjoyed these pictures. There were always several taped to the walls of our workroom. However, our concern here is not with the aesthetics and tastes of the adult, but rather with the problem of determining whether young children have a unique aesthetic sensitivity. Somewhat related to this is the question of whether young children can be taught, encouraged, or made aware of the beauty that exists around them.

Initially our studies were concerned with developmental differences in children's art; most of the work that children produced could be understood within a

163

developmental framework. As random scribbling or random brushstrokes give way to more organized and purposeful scribbles, the painting or drawing takes on form. As they begin to draw objects, children become more cautious about overlapping colors and pay attention to drawing and painting in empty spaces. Kindergarteners are careful to leave space around each of the objects. However, this developmental framework of children's art did not account for one interesting phenomenon. That is, occasionally children would paint blobs of color, or paint wiggly lines or some other pattern, long after they could draw recognizable objects. There seems to be an enjoyment of filling in areas with dots, repeating an interesting line pattern, or even balancing colors on the page. When nursery school children were questioned about the intent of these paintings, they would often respond with very

84. *Painting is sometimes done for nonrepresentational reasons, with concern for color, form, and balance. It could be argued that this aesthetic awareness is innate.*

direct but simple answers. A child would state that he was painting in red because he liked it, or that he was making a gooshy painting and that it goes goosh, goosh, goosh, goosh. Kindergarten children invariably responded with the comment that they were just making a design. It seemed that the word design meant any picture that did not have representational intent.

Young children do have an urge to paint or draw in ways that they think of as being pretty, beautiful, nice or aesthetically pleasing. But it should be emphasized that this interest in aesthetics is not contemplative because children did not change or alter their paintings once they were completed. Nor did they duplicate patterns or designs that appear on shirts, drapes, or wallpaper. Rather, the interest in putting down various colors or forms next to each other seemed to come primarily from an exploratory urge. Children knew when their picture satisfied them, but it was not on the basis of a careful evaluation of the elements in the picture itself. It seemed to be more involved with completing the process of painting and not a consideration of the elements that made up the picture.

It was particularly interesting to note how the use of color changed as children grew older. With two year olds the choice of color seems almost incidental as long as it contrasts with the paper. Our observations in the nursery school indicated that most young children mechanically paint a color directly over its container at the easel. But this application of the colors could be primarily to try out materials and a beginning step toward further exploration into the nature and quality of color. It was after the initial stage of getting acquainted with the tools and materials, and when there seemed to be no drive to put symbols on the paper, that the children began to contemplate the interrelationship of colors and forms. It was at this point that the painting took on a life of its own and was neither a record of a physical activity nor a record of symbol making. When paintings were made by six year olds, color was often used in what might be thought of as a documentary method. Those things that were green, such as trees, leaves, grass, and so forth, were painted green. There was no variation in the green itself, no indication of light and shade; the color was used primarily to document the information that certain things in the environment are green. Other colors were used in the same way; father's shirt was red, the sky blue, and so forth. Except for the designs, it was the younger children who had the greater amount of freedom in color use and who did not seem restricted by the real world in their selection of color.

We found examples of aesthetic pleasure in a variety of things besides paintings. Almost daily, children would stack up blocks for no apparent reason except the pleasure of seeing the finished structure, or a child would spend time letting sand run through his

85. *The feel of sand slipping through the fingers seems to be universally enjoyed by young children. This sensory experience is part of exploring the environment.*

fingers or watching the fish in the aquarium. Occasionally a child would get pleasure from looking at some paint that had spilled on the floor, watching the little stream of paint as it stopped and hardened. Clearly these were the kinds of activities that observers could not tabulate. We could not collect and sort these experiences, nor did we feel that children could explain why the sand was worth feeling, what was intriguing about the fish slowly moving through the water, or why it was important to watch paint run in interesting patterns and slowly change color as it dried. In this manner the child opened up a new direction for our thinking. From the harried adult point of view the sand was merely something which got on the floor, the aquarium was just another item in the nursery school, and the spilled paint was a nuisance to be cleaned up before it was tracked around the floor. This purely utilitarian approach that some adults took to these situations denied them the enjoyment the children were receiving. It is a rather sobering thought that perhaps adults need to be the learners rather than the teachers.

Exploratory behavior seems to be closely linked to aesthetic pleasure. In some cases it was hard to differentiate between these. A small child who puts her finger in a puddle of water and watches the ripples could be said to exhibit exploratory behavior and scientific curiosity to detemine the result of the action upon the surface of the water, but it might also be an aesthetic experience as she watched the ripples grow larger and finally subside. Possibly when we describe some of this contemplative behavior, we should not consider it purely as aesthetic sensitivity, because we are talking about the child's fascination and curiosity with a changing and enlarging environment.

Developmental Stages

We have been discussing the meaning of aesthetics for young children as seen through our observations. There is some experimental evidence for aesthetic awareness. Holladay (1966) found that when three year old children were scribbling on a piece of paper on which was a darkened rectangle, they would make their marks outside, or inside, or would draw around that grayed area. However, children a year younger would ignore minor variations on the surfaces and would just scribble on the paper as a whole. This awareness of another shape, and altering scribbling patterns to accommodate it, could be considered as the beginning of aesthetic judgment. At this age a child is sufficiently aware of shapes to be able to select a square from a series of geometric forms (Brittain, 1969). However, this ability does not imply that he has a fully developed visual memory, since most three year old children do not recognize their own paintings the following day; in fact, even four year olds have difficulty at that task. Apparently visual memory develops slowly.

When nursery school children look at pictures, either in a storybook or one that has been put up for them to enjoy, they can usually identify objects in these pictures. Sometimes a man is called Daddy, or a dog is called by their pet dog's name. There seems to be no understanding of any action that is depicted in the picture, nor is the theme or artist's intent noticed in any way. Rather, children enumerate what they see and are satisfied with that. Even kindergarten children do not go much further than this. Although they can identify colors in pictures if these colors are not too subtle, there is no feeling for the interaction or interrelationship between the parts of the picture. These findings are in agreement with a separate study in England by Vernon (1965), who has indicated from her research that it is not until ten or eleven years of age that children can interpret what is happening in a picture, what the people are doing, or what action is taking place. And it seems that it is not until a child reaches junior high school that he begins to sense the mood or atmosphere of a picture (Brittain, 1968).

When we asked children whether they liked a particular picture, their likes and dislikes were determined on a very personal note. That is, if the object portrayed had a familiar and favorable connotation to the child, it was liked. One picture of a baking scene was liked because "I like cookies." Another scene with a dog was liked because "that looks like Ruffy."

And still another with flowers was liked because "flowers are pretty." It seemed clear with the nursery school children that the word *like* was not so much an aesthetic judgment as it was a word synonymous with good, pretty, nice, which extended to food, friends, home, and so forth.

In a study conducted at Pennsylvania State University (Liedes, 1975), the qualities of beauty and ugliness as determined by six year old children were examined in detail. Children were asked to bring to school objects that they thought were pretty and some objects that they thought were ugly. Also, children were asked to sort 126 pictures into three groups: beautiful, ugly, and not sure. In less than half the pictures did 50 per cent or more of the children agree whether it was beautiful or not. This certainly shows that there is no common agreement among six year old children as to what constitutes beauty. However,

86. There is a certain aesthetic honesty in painting the inside of a box, even if no one will see the color after it is completed.

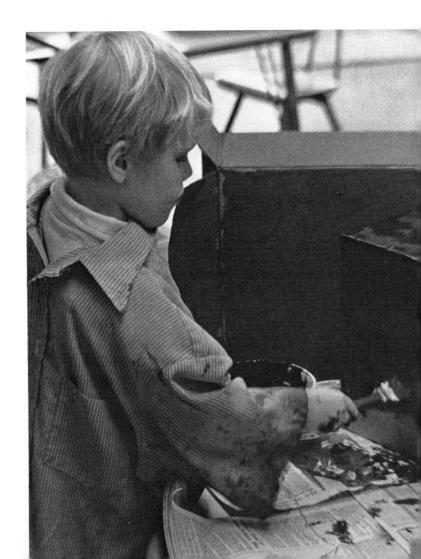

those pictures that most children agreed were beautiful contained flowers, animals, home furnishings, jewelry, birds, and other familiar objects. All were comfortable, pleasurable items in the child's experience. The ugly pictures tended to be those that contained skeletons, human skulls, a Frankenstein, guns, and so forth. It should be mentioned that all of the pictures were brought in originally by the children and therefore had some relevance to the population.

In our observations and discussions with children in the Cornell Nursery School, we were occasionally shown treasures that children had safely stashed away in their pockets. These included a pencil stub, a particular marble, a small plastic toy, and a special doll that was brought to school. It was enough for the child to recognize that you saw this prized object, and then it was put away again. The children obviously placed value on these items; in some cases it seemed as if it took a bit of courage to show these to adults. For the most part these items were not shared with peers. Why these particular items were treasured is difficult to fathom, but there evidently was an individual value system beginning to operate that was not based upon monetary considerations or upon adult standards.

Aesthetic Preferences of Teachers

As we mentioned earlier, the teachers in charge of nursery schools and kindergartens were responsible for any pleasing arrangement of still life or display of pictures on the walls. In some cases we saw vases of flowers, a careful display of pictures of musical instruments, and even a changing exhibit of modern art that supposedly would appeal to children, such as works by Paul Klee and Marc Chagall. However, the children were apt to be completely oblivious to these external decorations. They seemed to be more influenced by the overt actions of the teacher, when certain of their drawings or paintings were customarily selected as being nice, when approval was given for certain types of work, and when some of these pictures were displayed on bulletin boards or in the halls. There were even instances when some of the art projects seemed to be designed primarily to give children a lesson in aesthetics, or at least in some of the elements of balance, harmony, or color relations. We saw dittoed sheets that consisted of circles or squares supposedly nicely balanced on a page for children to color with specific colors of crayons. Sometimes there would be flowers precut from construction paper for the children to put together and paste on a sheet of paper to make a pretty picture. But *pretty* in this case was clearly determined by the teacher. The observers felt that in some cases the treasures that children stored in their pockets would not be shared with the teacher because there was obviously a discrepancy in aesthetic values.

Sensory Considerations

In a broad sense the question of aesthetic sensitivity can be seen as one facet of a child's changing relationship to his environment. What a child selects and cherishes stems from personal feelings and to some extent is hidden from the rest of the world. How adults react to works of art may very well be influenced by their experiences in early childhood. Aesthetics cannot be taught. An understanding adult can listen to children and be sensitive to their likes and dislikes, but he cannot make these choices for them.

It is through the senses that we can understand and try to deal with our environment. This may sound like an obvious statement, but it is easily forgotten in working with young children. They enjoy looking at, feeling, smelling, listening to, and tasting all sorts of things which may seem absurd to adults. But it is only through this first-hand contact with the environment that the young child learns. Parents sometimes seem to be particularly worried about the process of touching, smelling, and tasting. Any store at any time will usually have at least one parent in it who is telling the

child, "Don't touch, keep your hands off." Apparently looking is a much safer thing to do. The child may often be admonished: Keep your hands clean, put down that dirty bug, what do you have in your mouth now, can't you leave things alone, why are you always getting into things, put that down right now; but young children need to actively explore the world around them. It is only later that the eyes can recognize that which has been explored with all of the senses. It is rather surprising then to find that, as early as kindergarten, learning has become almost entirely visual in nature. Pictures are substituted for the real thing, and the assumption is that the bigger the picture the better. And of course words become much more the means by which the academic subjects are taught; whatever first-hand sensory experience the child may have acquired before attending school has to suffice as a basis for understanding these pictures and words.

It is now well documented that damage can be done when an infant is isolated and removed from sensory stimulation. Having objects to look at and manipulate, or having a mobile over a crib is now accepted practice. In our discussions with nursery school teachers we found that one reason for including a number of art activities was to reinforce the child's sensory experiences. At one point we attempted to make a list of materials that were used in art projects. However, we soon abandoned that notion when we found that almost anything and everything was used at some point or other, depending in part upon the teacher. This included such things as packing materials, junked electronic parts, eggshells, burned-out light bulbs, and so forth. Most of these materials merely provided a tactile experience, rather than a fully sensory experience, which was the reason given for these projects. They included having children touch or feel mushy or sticky substances such as soap flakes beaten to a frothy mass, sawdust added to paste for some kind of manipulation, and a mixture of flour, salt, and water for children to pat and fondle. It was as if this were a necessary part of the curriculum, a preparation for an adult life of squishing and mushing which could not be left to chance.

87. The mysteries of his world are explored by a preschooler in his play. He needs nobody to make explanations; he makes his own discoveries.

It was interesting to note that some of these same teachers became upset when youngsters got dirty playing outside; or when the official sensory time was over, they checked to make sure that hands were clean, everything was picked up, and the environment was sterile again. We found this rather strange, because these same children were touching, looking at, manipulating, and collecting pieces of interesting junk or a captured bug or moth. Yet these collections were often dismissed as irrelevant, whereas the planned sen-

88. Somehow it seems all right to get sticky and mushy when the activity is called art. Some teachers feel this type of sensory experience is important.

sory activity incorporated into the daily schedule was thought to be an important part of the education of these children. The point here is that a special sensory time seems ridiculous; in a number of cases the natural inclination of children to touch, compare, manipulate, weigh, and handle objects could be included as part of the natural interaction between children and adults without the artificial isolation of this experience as a prescribed part of the day.

Perception and Understanding

When we speak of perception we usually think about visual perception. What and how we see influences all of our actions. There is the point of view that young children need to learn to see; the evidence indicates that young children see the same thing as adults do, since this is primarily a biological function. However, the fact that young eyes receive the same retinal impression does not mean that the young mind deals with the information received in the same way as adults would. There is no straight line progression from seeing and vaguely understanding some diagram to a good understanding of the same diagram with accurate estimations of proportion, size relationships, and line direction. It has been shown that sometimes this will work in opposite directions; that is, young children will give better judgments of line length than will older children (Piaget, 1969). What the child knows sometimes gets in the way of what he sees. A more accurate visual representation of a person will be drawn by a kindergarten child before attention is focused upon particular body parts. We showed kindergarten children their image in a full length mirror and had them draw themselves with their own images as reference. A comparison of these drawings with unmotivated drawings showed that an increased awareness of detail also produced greater distortion. In a study with somewhat older children, Lewis (1963) found that drawings of houses by kindergarten children tended to be more naturalistically correct than did those of children in first, second, and third grades.

These older children were concerned about drawing several sides of a house, which would be impossible to view naturally. It seems then that the perceptual image a child receives is valuable only in how he deals with this information.

We have already discussed in Chapter 4 some of the experiments on the ability of children to copy geometric forms. It was found that the youngest children, those of two and three years of age, did not look at the square or triangle after they started to copy it. Older children did look back to check the accuracy of

89. (*Below*) *The most important thing in eating is the teeth. Such distortions are common and are not a perceptual misunderstanding of proportion.*

90. *A six year old girl drew this picture of herself sleeping. She has emphasized her feet, necessary for kicking aside the blankets.*

their copy during the process, although the same instructions were given to all children. The ability to pay attention to distinctive features of a form is related to success in copying that form. However, the opposite point of view could also be stated: when a child is no longer satisfied with merely making an enclosed shape for a triangle, he will check the distinctive features; possibly his understanding of the form precedes his perceptual awareness of the details of that form.

Trying to use children's drawings as a step toward increasing their perceptual awareness has certain drawbacks. First it should be remembered that young children expect everyone to see things as they do. This

177

is an egocentric stage; pointing out that their drawings are not correct, or that the object really does not look the way it is drawn, merely criticizes a child on a basis that he does not understand. For the young child, his drawings represent things as they are; it is not the problems of perception that adults should worry about, but the problem of intellectual functioning. What children see and how they understand what they see is a complex problem which cannot be dealt with on a superficial level. Some of the kindergarten

91. The reason for this lesson is to promote perceptual awareness of geometric forms. Experience in handling these forms must precede their comprehension, and their recognition when seen on a two-dimensional surface.

178

teachers with whom we talked planned particular art activities for the development of perceptual abilities. Sometimes these exercises were a part of a commercial program for reading readiness. "Color all the big circles red, color all the little circles green." "Find all the triangles and color them blue." What is sad about this attempt at improving perceptual abilities is that these programs and exercises are of no value. We observed some children coloring geometric forms very laboriously, some putting a dash of color here and there to satisfy the teacher. One child who was having problems was scribbling all over the page; he was doomed. What makes this even more ironic was that all of the children could easily have told the teacher which of two balls were larger if they had been asked that question.

Children in kindergarten usually have no trouble in distinguishing between larger and smaller, taller

92. *Asking children to spend time coloring in certain triangles red and others blue, with the hope that it will teach triangle recognition, will not promote perceptual awareness.*

(From "Things You See" TAE for levels 3, 4, and 5, Macmillan Reading Program. Albert J. Harris and Mae Knight Clark, senior authors. Copyright 1974 by Macmillan Publishing Co.)

PRACTICE EXERCISE

Direct the pupils: Color each part of the design the right color.
Use your Color Chart to find out the color words, if you need to.

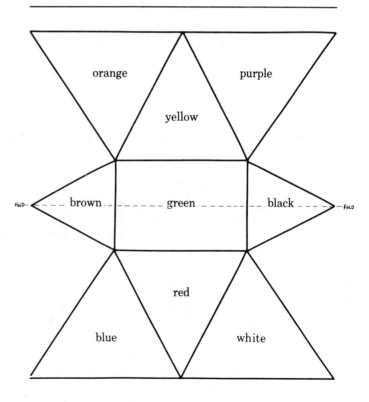

and shorter, as long as the objects compared are real. Even retarded children seem to have little difficulty in that task. In a study using groups of retarded children matched with normal children of three, five, and seven years of age, Pawlikowski (1978) found that differences between how these groups of children responded depended upon whether they were shown pictures or real objects. In one instance all the retarded children were readily able to select the bigger of two balls only a moment before failing a test to identify the bigger of two circles drawn in black ink on a piece of white cardboard. Since all these children received the same physical impression on the retina of the eye, it must be that the transference of the three-dimensional world onto a two-dimensional surface creates some kinds of problems. These problems are not perceptual in the usual sense but are tied to a mode of thinking. Certainly, increasing the number of coloring-in exercises for kindergarten youngsters who have trouble with this type of activity will only create additional problems, particularly when we realize that the child may already know the concept that the teacher is trying to teach. There is enough in the literature to show that anxiety reduces accuracy in perceptual tasks, so that the child essentially has two strikes against him if he cannot do the task, and is bored if he can.

Coordination of Perspectives

There are some perceptual tasks that are not possible for kindergarten children to master, and impossible for nursery school children to attempt. One of these is taking someone else's viewpoint. Some of the original work in this area was referred to as the coordination of perspectives (Piaget and Inhelder, 1967). Three pasteboard mountains are shown on a table; the child is shown some pictures and asked to pick out the view that he sees. This is not difficult, but when asked to pick out the picture that the doll on the opposite side of the table sees, or the view from the child's left or right, the task becomes incomprehensible. Substituting some tableware for the mountains, Hooper (1977) found that even 90 per cent of the second graders she tested could not pick out the proper view that a toy bear would see from different places at the table. Hooper also found that when second, fourth, and sixth grade children were asked to draw a table, these drawings increased in accuracy of portraying three dimensions, which paralleled the youngster's ability to successfully take a viewpoint other than his own. It appears that this is more a cognitive task than a perceptual one. However, some kindergarten teachers plan art projects for a child in which he is supposed to draw the school-yard from the viewpoint of a bird, or play the role of a Pilgrim, or manipulate a puppet as if he were someone else.

Attention and Perceptual Awareness

Closely related to the problems of perception is the child's span of attention. For the most part children attend to those things which are of interest to them, and there are varying degrees of interest in things that are suggested or displayed by teachers. It seems logical, from our experience in observing children, that the most economical method of increasing perceptual awareness is to build upon the child's own concerns and interests and to try to expand or refine these. Children bring into school found objects which can be looked at and discussed. Often the painting process provides ample opportunity for the development of perceptual sensitivity by extending the child's frame of reference and encouraging the interaction of the child with his own experiences, and by making these experiences more explicit by encouraging comparisons, emphasizing differences, and stressing such things as color and texture. Even a very young child who is drawing a scribble of Daddy can be perceptually motivated by extending his frame of reference. "Is your Daddy taller than you are, does he have rough whiskers, does he hold you up high, does he wear glasses, does he have big feet, do you like him?"

Sometimes one such question is enough; in other instances, children make no verbal response but change the drawing by including additional scribbles as a means of response.

The development of perceptual awareness is a crucial part of learning. However, we must remember that children may not view the world as we do, and it is only through a child's understanding of what he sees that growth can take place.

93. *The drawing process demands that children organize and consolidate perceptual impressions. They have no need to imitate adult stereotypes.*

9

Art and Cognitive Growth

Importance of Art Activity

Young children constantly interact physically with their environment. This interaction takes the form of touching, looking at, listening to, smelling, and even tasting anything and everything around. This constant interaction with the environment provides the basis for the child's understanding of his world and is a necessary part of his development. Our thesis is that the production of art provides one of the best ways for a preschool child to understand, organize, and utilize concepts.

In watching children drawing and painting in numerous contexts, the observers became aware of the fact that the children who drew and painted the most were those who could do this well. This might be

183

considered natural, since the practice of a particular skill is considered one way of becoming proficient in that skill. However, drawing and painting may be a good deal more than just skills, and could be an excellent means of facilitating cognitive development, the means through which a child organizes his concepts so that they become understandable to him and become assimilated into his intellectual functioning. But we need to be more specific.

It was pointed out in Chapter 4 that one of the attributes of children who were able to do copying tasks more advanced for their age than expected was their interest and involvement in art activities. It was also noted that even very young children who drew or had the opportunity to scribble with crayons were at an advanced state of scribbles compared with those children who did not have such opportunities. It has also been shown (Harris, 1963) that there is a positive relationship between the number of details included in a drawing and the intellectual ability of children. In fact, the relationship between art ability and intellectual ability is both strong and positive up until about the age of ten (Burkhart, 1967).

Art is primarily considered an expressive medium. The act of drawing or painting is looked upon as an external expression of an inner state, both intellectually and emotionally. It has therefore been assumed that if a child develops cognitively beyond his years, he will express this same development in his art products. Our belief is that the art activities do more than just reflect the inner child; they help to form it.

The drawing, whether by a scribbling child or by one who is drawing recognizable objects, is basically a symbol of an event. This event becomes characterized in concrete terms, in tangible visible terms, for the drawing serves as more than a reminder of the event; it is also a means of clarifying and organizing the event in such a way as to make recall of the event more accessible. From an adult's point of view, what is drawn may seem somewhat incidental. The drawing usually indicates some particular relationship between the child and an object, such as his house, pet, family members, or whatever. Or it may be a representation of some kinesthetic activity, as we observed when the child was drawing a dog running, or eating fast. In such a case it does not have a reference to a visible object or activity. However, the opportunity to portray the event becomes a means of categorizing or filing the event into the existing framework of the mind, and concretizing the event in such a way that it can be used later as a basis for future action or for comparison. There is no need for the drawing to resemble the house or the family members; what is important is that the features that distinguish the event are important and meaningful to the child and thus distinguishable from other objects or experiences.

The complex array of features that differentiate one event from another cannot be dealt with verbally at an age when verbal ability is limited. However, the drawing provides the means by which characteristic features, whatever is necessary for connoting a person or house, can be put down in what amounts to a sort

94. *A drawing by a six year old shows the essence of a rainstorm as it surrounds the house, with the occupants safe inside.*

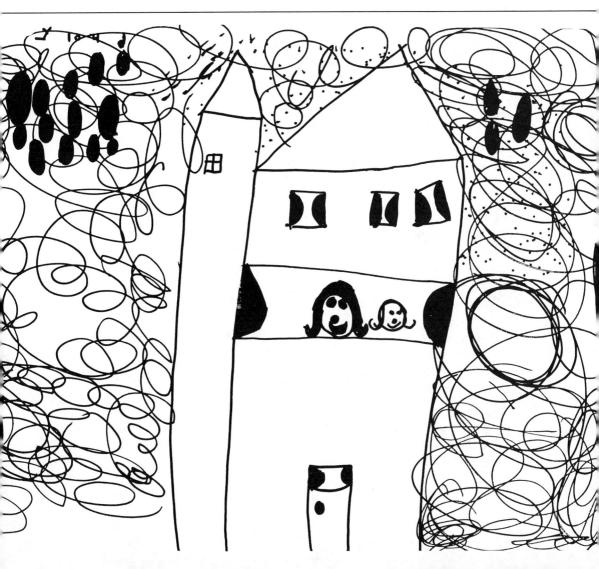

of shorthand. The drawing therefore takes on the role of a symbol which becomes both a record of an object or event and also a record of the process of assimilation of that information.

Factors Influencing Art Ability

How a drawing is made obviously depends upon many factors. Most important of these is the mental age of the child. The amount of information with which a child can deal varies in quantity and kind as the child grows. This corresponds roughly with chronological age, but we have seen where this can be advanced or retarded.

A second factor is the degree of awareness the child has at the time he is drawing. This awareness of the event or object is the result of the recall of that event at the time he is drawing. This is a crucial element in that it may be possible for adults to increase this ability, this degree of awareness. We have mentioned that when we talked with children, they increased the length of time they spent in drawing, and their drawings became more elaborate. A discussion of the subject being drawn, a house or family members, can also increase the awareness that a child has of that subject. Because children accept the world as it is, it might be possible for a child to passively notice enough of the environment to escape harm and avoid unpleasant situations. This seems to be the case with some children who are considered to be disadvantaged. Passivity was a characteristic of those who had difficulty in copying geometric forms. However, children, like most of the animal kingdom, have a natural tendency to explore; they are curious and are attracted to the unusual. The fact that some of these explorations and discoveries about the environment can be recorded provides a means by which these experiences become internalized.

One of the striking things that impressed us when young children were copying geometric forms was the fact that the model was not referred to in the copying process except for the initial recognition. This is cer-

95. *This painting shows the child's concepts and an awareness of his environment. Notice that he has moved around his painting to work at it from the top.*

tainly true when children are painting or drawing in school. Their drawings may be composed of people, but rarely does a child stop to look at anyone as a reference for the drawing itself. It is as if the child views the real world in a selective way; his drawings reflect that which is vital to the child himself. In the example of copying geometric forms, it seemed that the child used the model merely as a recall agent and produced his internal image rather than confronting directly that which he was drawing or trying to represent. Possibly there is no mental image until the child makes one.

There is no question in our minds; the child is not drawing the external environment. His drawings

187

show the visually impossible, but this is perfectly satisfactory to the child. He will draw the legs of a table
spreading out in all directions, he will draw objects
floating in space, or make things with sides so that we
can see through them as if we had X-ray vision. The
drawing a child produces may show little likeness to
the object he is making, and the child himself can recognize these discrepancies.

A five year old child may copy a simplified drawing of a house, and it will be somewhat like the original. However, if he copies a real house, the drawing
will bear little resemblance to the original. This makes
us acutely aware of the fact that children's thinking
abilities have not yet developed sufficiently to be able
to organize elements that they see into a cohesive
whole. This is not to say that there is not a cohesive

96. *This child may have
trouble making stars ac-
cording to a formula, but
there is no problem in
showing the family sitting
around the table. This
top view of the table
allows us to see each in-
dividual place setting.*

whole from the child's point of view, but rather that from an adult's point of view the elements that go to make up the real house are not organized spatially to the extent that they become parts of a total picture. In copying a house from an adult's picture, the child merely has to duplicate what is in front of him, which is more a mechanical process, but we are not interested in training very many of our young children to become duplicating machines.

It is through the process of touching, holding, and feeling parts of his world that a youngster gets an understanding of the tactile or textural qualities and the notion of substance and three-dimensionality. Through the process of looking at, manipulating, examining in detail, and seeing relationships of size and shape, an understanding of objects and space is formed. These are external methods of exploring and

97. *A child needs to manipulate, explore, and investigate extensively. A sterile environment may be orderly but uninspiring.*

understanding the environment, however; it is only through the cognitive processes, the ability to assimilate some of this information through a larger framework of memory and understanding, that we can say that any learning takes place. It is this interactive process between the child and the environment that is crucial. Merely exposing children to a variety of experiences will not automatically produce a greater depth of understanding or greater awareness of environment unless the mental processes can and do assimilate this information into a usable framework.

In looking at children's drawings, it is easy to see that the first stage of development is basically sensorimotor in origin. That is, the child is operating in a direct way, using the crayon at first to put down random marks and later coordinated ones. This moves rapidly into another stage, at about the age of three, when these scribbling lines begin to stand for something. They represent movement not of the crayon itself but of objects in the environment. However, adults usually think of representation as being visual representation which starts at about the age of four, as we have already discussed. This early kind of representation is not a copy of things as they are; the child is not yet able to deal with proper proportions, relationship of parts, or even to put things in proper sequence or order. Rather, his drawings reflect first a differentiation between space and an object. The closed form which is separated from the rest of the page becomes a person, a house, or something else. These forms are constantly changing, and the child will make objects larger or smaller depending in part on the space available on the paper. It is of no consequence that the head is larger than the body. When young children copied geometric forms we saw that they tended to make a closed form, like a circle, for both the square and the triangle. The hand is shown as a closed form, but the fingers are lines added to the hand, although not necessarily the right number. What seems most important to the youngster at this stage of development is the separation of one object from another.

The first indication of order is seen within the framework of an individual object. For example, the drawing of a man will be shown with the head on top

98. *This mailman looks as if he were walking on a sidewalk, an unusual concept for a six year old; but by the end of kindergarten most children do have a base line upon which their drawings rest.*

of a body, the arms will stick out from each side, and the legs will protrude downward from the bottom of the body. It is only later, at about five years of age, that there begins to be some semblance of order in the total drawing. Here the order seems based upon an imaginary line at the bottom of the page upon which all of the objects begin to be placed. It is not until about six or seven years of age that there is a definite baseline and that a schema develops for drawing a person or a house or whatever. We find that there is consistency in the way children draw, and now proportion, order, and placement become important. But, as we saw in Chapter 8, each object may be drawn from a different viewpoint as if the child himself is still involved in an egocentric view of each object and cannot take an objective point of view of his subject matter.

These stages pretty much follow Piaget's stages of development, of the child's understanding of space (Piaget and Inhelder, 1967). The first stage, up to the age of four or five, is referred to as topological space, which is followed by projective and Euclidean space. It is not until about the age of nine that projective space is understood, and it is even later before children begin to have some feeling for depth and perspective in their own drawings.

We have seen that the organization of space in a child's drawing follows his developmental process.

99. There is a lot going on in this drawing. Notice the amount of detail: cupboards, a plant on what may be the television, lights in the ceiling, and people in the next room.

The process of organizing space is an intellectual function. As the child sees size relationships, understands locational relationships, and develops proportional relationships, he develops abstract thinking. The organization of space is relative to an organization of time too, and often one sees, within a single drawing, the lumping together of events that take place at different times or locations. The organization of space, the development of structure, and the increased awareness and ability to represent the environment are basic elements in the problem-solving tasks that confront the child in drawing or painting. It is the interrelationship between these and the subject matter he is trying to portray that help in the child's cognitive understanding of the environment.

Learning in the Art Process

We have been discussing art activities, particularly drawing and painting, as a means by which a child can organize and conceptualize the environment and deal with it in a meaningful way. However, there is another aspect to the art experience that is important to consider. The value of art is not just in the portrayal of events, or just in attempts at reproducing significant parts of a child's environment; rather, a good deal of learning takes place in the art itself. We discussed this somewhat in our consideration of the role of aesthetics as related to young children, but it is part of cognitive growth.

The process of drawing requires a set of continual interactions. Once a line is drawn on a blank piece of paper the child reacts to it. His next line therefore is influenced by what is already done, and the process of putting down the third, fourth, and further lines are all dependent upon what is already on the paper. In some cases the youngster reacts to the visual message that is received, and we have records of three year olds responding with a gleeful "Look what I made." However, sometimes it is not the visual message that is important, but merely the experience and pleasure in putting down lines and forms that are a record of

the child's having been there. This is a means by which a child not only has some influence on the external world but also makes a record for others to see, thus helping to define his own identity as an individual.

The child, in altering the surface of the paper and in modifying his drawing actions, creates a new pattern incorporating information based upon past

100. (Above) One thing that is a real struggle at this age is learning to tie shoes.

194

experiences and present action. Each drawing is different, yet over a period of time a child shows a more highly organized and more highly developed awareness both of what is drawn and of the physical actions required for the drawing act. The act of drawing is a dynamic activity, based in part upon the internal reactions of a child to the drawing itself.

Although we are discussing drawing and painting, the same would hold true for working with clay or other three-dimensional constructions. Building form upon form, watching it collapse, looking through space or holes in a construction, adding pieces here or there, or smashing the whole thing flat again would provide many opportunities for seeing one's self as responsible for the creation and destruction of a unique form. This interaction is both visual and haptic in nature. In this active construction, exchanges between the child and the object take place.

101. *Sometimes it takes a little help from a friend.*

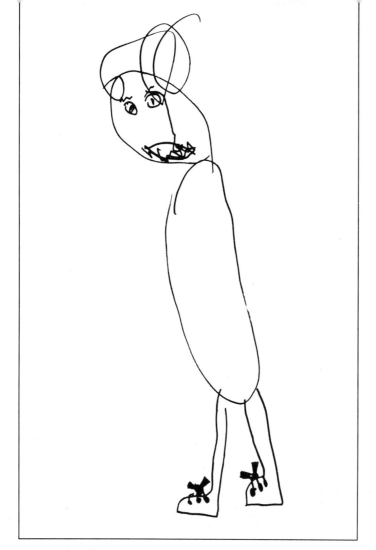

102. (Left) When you
learn to tie shoes, shoe-
laces become important
to include in your
drawing.

We have mentioned several times that art activities are a serious matter for children. There seems to
be a challenge, not so much in mastering the materials, as in mastering the concepts that a child is trying
to portray. This is hard work. It is interesting to note
that children enjoy the art activities in spite of the
efforts involved. If fun or enjoyment were a child's
prime motivation for using art materials, then one
could expect a greater length of time would be spent
on those activities that are easy to do, are somehow
frivolous in nature, or take the form of games. Such
has not been the case. Dripping paint on paper, pasting sunflower seeds on to cardboard, or paddling
around with finger paint on their feet, all novel ideas
to the children, tended to be treated in a somewhat

103. (Right) Young
children work very
seriously on their paint-
ings. Sometimes it takes
two brushes to master the
materials.

bored fashion by the participants. These activities were quickly dismissed, occasionally in favor of a pencil and piece of paper.

Support for the notion that children derive pleasure from challenges in cognitive mastery comes from a study at Yale University (Harter, 1974); although work was done with fifth and sixth grade youngsters, the study indicated that maximum gratification was derived from solving challenging problems, whereas easily-solved problems provided relatively little pleasure for these children. We certainly have evidence that for young children the same holds true; that is, nursery school and kindergarten children actively sought out challenging art experiences and enjoyed the mastery of tasks which they set for themselves.

We need to know a great deal more about how children learn. However, the evidence that we have secured makes us realize the importance of art in the development of cognitive abilities. There is something exciting for children in the organizing and abstracting process which is a necessary part of producing art. This is not a passive activity, but one which encompasses all of the senses, each providing some input into an operational system which creates new forms that are constantly altered through an interaction process. The activity of bringing together and elaborating upon the essence of the external world, coupled with the physical activity of exploring through the use of color, form, and space, provides an opportunity to develop a reality which in a broad sense could be considered knowledge.

104. *The teacher probably did not reward or even notice Dougy's creative drawings of three interesting trees, four different houses, six varieties of balls, eight dancing balloons, seven umbrellas with different handles, or five types of bottles.*

Art in the Academic Program

Closely related to a youngster's cognitive development is his success in school. Success is usually measured in terms of grades received in academic subjects — reading, writing, and arithmetic. Somehow the arts do not play an important part in whether a youngster is promoted from one grade to another. The notion of working hard and doing well does not apply to drawing and painting; there seems to be the general

Name Dougy

Write the number:

2

4

3

5

1

6

8

7

9

10

Draw 4 [houses] and 3 [tree]s.

Draw 6 [ball]'s and 8 [balloon]'s

Draw 7 [umbrella]'s and 5 [bottle]'s

attitude that unless one has a talent for the arts there isn't much that a youngster can do, or for that matter the teacher either, to increase the quality of the work produced. Because there are often problems with extrinsic rewards, it is just as well that art can be left unevaluated, particularly at the nursery school and kindergarten levels.

However, art is often used as the means to sugarcoat other subject matter. Because children enjoy drawing and painting, one often finds a lot of the reading, writing, and arithmetic programs concealed in many art-type activities that children perform. We have mentioned the use of worksheets where children are expected to color a certain number of kites green, or where the proper color is supposed to be put over all the diamonds or triangles but not on the squares and circles. It is no wonder that the child's enthusiasm for art is given a severe blow.

The use of art in this way might conceivably be justified by those advocates of a strong reading, writing, and arithmetic program if there were some evidence that these exercises actually are of value. The evidence does not exist. There seems to be almost a fear of letting children work through a problem, or develop concepts on their own. Are teachers trying to protect children from failure when they provide them with coloring exercises? Or are the teachers protecting themselves? It would be understandable if some children feel that we do not trust them to think. There is no reason to have children trace, copy, or color in, except to give the kindergarten teacher a few minutes' rest.

Reading, Writing, Arithmetic, and Art

Often the kindergarten class is expected to develop reading readiness skills so that when children arrive in first grade they can start in on a serious reading program. The problems of illiteracy within our society are well known and there is some concern that schools may not be doing their job properly. However, what constitutes reading readiness is somewhat debatable. In fact, there may even be a question raised: What is reading? The usual definition seems to be that of recognizing the visual shapes of words and being able to decode these and translate them into oral language. It may be that this is the goal toward which teachers strive, but it may actually have very little to do with literacy. Reading and writing should be seen as tools and not ends in themselves. The mere recognition of letters, or letters grouped to make words, does not necessarily mean that the child understands or can utilize the information which has been decoded. Reading implies more than merely understanding the meaning of individual words; reading should be able to evoke thoughts, questions, and interpretations. The written word needs to be related to the experience of the reader so that inferences can be drawn, a critical evaluation of what is written can be made, and what is read can be related to the actual experiences of the child. To prepare in kindergarten for that kind of reading program would mean that attention should be focused on the exchange of information, on the organization of thoughts, and on the assimilation of experiences. Time spent in trying to develop particular skills, such as recognizing letters or learning the alphabet, may actually have very little to do with interpreting written material.

Certainly some of the work that we undertook in having children copy squares and triangles shows that it is better to wait until the youngster can do these tasks successfully than to frustrate him with tasks that he cannot yet accomplish. We noticed that children, when asked to write their names on drawings, tended to make their names in much the same fashion as the drawing itself. That is, if the child is scribbling, the make-believe writing would also look like scribbles. However, when the child begins to draw recognizable objects and sees the line as a symbol for something else, attempts at writing his name also begin to assume a definite form and shape. Perhaps the best way to teach writing would be to have children draw and paint, to give them the opportunity to develop the skills necessary to accomplish the task at their own pace. It would be frustrating for a child who has not yet seen the line as connoting a symbol, to be suddenly confronted with a mass of lines that are sup-

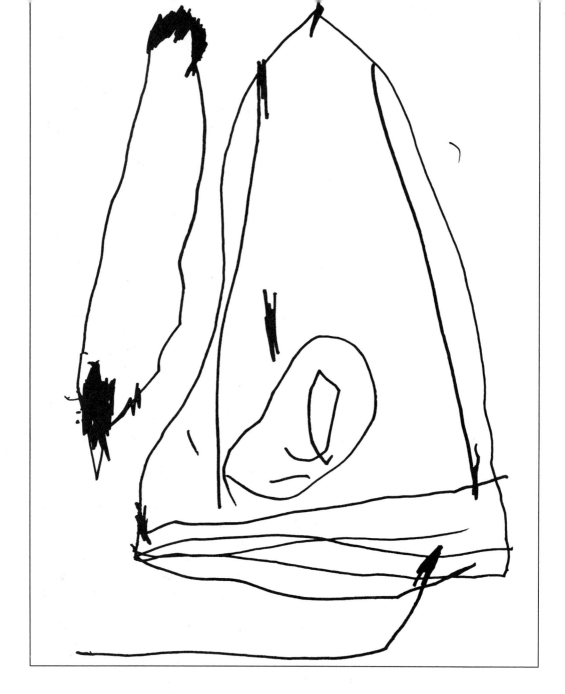

posed to connote some sort of meaning; adults would
recognize these lines immediately as the word for cow
or hat or whatever. To think that these squiggles
could actually be a symbol for an object which is not
present is a real discovery. Certainly children who
have not made this discovery themselves in their own
drawings would have difficulty seeing written words
as conveying meaning.

105. *This three year old is far from being able to copy letters. He is able to form closed shapes which have meaning only for himself.*

202

We have mentioned that drawings can sometimes give a better indication of a child's reading readiness than a teacher's estimate can. Drawings are often used as indicators of a child's intellectual development. We found that children who drew a good deal were better at this task than children who did not draw very much. Putting these three statements together, one is immediately confronted with the possibility that art should be considered more than an amusing pastime for children at nursery school and kindergarten levels.

Sometimes particular programs are utilized to help children get ready to learn how to read. We will discuss one of these programs in more detail in Chapter 10 but all of the specific attributes that are considered necessary in a reading readiness program may actually bear little relationship to reading itself. Trying to increase children's visual discrimination, trying to refine a child's understanding of spatial relations, or trying to develop a child's visual-motor integration, with the hope that putting these three components together will be a good background for reading comprehension, is basically unjustified. Even such things as memory, auditory discrimination, and eye-hand coordination are all isolated factors which individually appear to be unrelated to academic success. It is interesting to note that there are numerous tests on the market to ascertain a child's disability in each of these areas, but the test makers have little in the way of justification for their wares (Livingston, 1972; Larsen & Hammill, 1975; Larsen, Rogers, & Sowell, 1976).

Although we think of certain subject matter as being academic, not all learning in this area takes place in the classroom. The socioeconomic status of the family is one of the best predictors of the child's eventual success in learning to read and write. Trying to document just why this condition exists is difficult, but the availability of an interested adult provides a clue. We found that in talking with children about their drawings, youngsters communicated their thoughts and ideas to an adult listener, using the drawing as a reference point. This use of a drawing as a means of communication is often overlooked. It should be stated honestly that the communication we saw when young children drew was not a discourse between the child and the attentive adult but rather a communication of a child with himself. That is, the marks on the page often were shorthand notations of an event, or in some cases were seen by the child as resembling or symbolizing something in his environment. In a sense the child was reading his own picture, using his own words and his own experiences as references. There is a cognitive process involved in acquiring the basic skills necessary for reading. A good deal of the work that has been done to date has concentrated on the mechanics of reading; little is really understood about how children learn this process.

In talking to and working with young children, we have been constantly impressed by the individuality of each child. Each youngster expresses himself in different ways; sometimes we found that youngsters have different meanings for the same words. Although in a broad sense the drawings and paintings by preschool children fall into certain categories, the variation within these categories is tremendous. It seemed a little sad to us that the nursery school children would soon be confronted with a formal school setting that operates under a policy of everyone doing the same thing at the same time.

There seems to be no advantage for children to be taught to read early. Some countries delay this process until a later age. For some children it may be better to have no reading program than to have one that is designed to cure what are interpreted as disabilities. Learning to read is a complex process, and too often we forget that motivation can play a central role in this process. A youngster must not only be "ready," he must also be eager to find out what the symbols mean and try to translate the written word into a meaningful piece of information. Words are not isolated abstract forms to be memorized but are rather indicators of experience that need a reference point in the child's life.

Although we have been discussing reading and writing, number concepts fall into the same framework. Just because a child can count does not necessarily mean that he understands what counting means. Number names are nonsense words which gradually take on several meanings. These can be a quantity, a

106. *Leah has learned
to make letters while
fairly young. These were
somehow learned without
formal instruction and
are closely related to an
interest in drawing.*

point in a series, a name of an interesting shape, and
so on. Most children learn how to count before they
arrive in kindergarten, so there is no reason to dwell
on rote memorization or to draw innumerable birds
or kites to demonstrate this skill. However, all kindergarteners believe, and with good reason, that five
elephants are more than five mice. Nursery school
children are sometimes very careful about counting
five fingers as they draw them, and even the first representations of a person clearly have two eyes and two
legs. Children spontaneously sort and arrange blocks;

clay is often rolled into balls and counted or even grouped into large and small. Arithmetic is not learned only as a result of formal instruction.

The relationship between drawing and writing is obvious. Both are expressive, both communicate, and both need the development of comparable skills. There is enough evidence to support the hypothesis that a good foundation for a reading program is creative art activity. To take away such activity or, worse, to substitute unthinking coloring exercises, deprives the child of the opportunity to establish his own relationship to his environment or to make his own discoveries of form and shape, and negates the very basis of a good reading program: the self-identification with symbols which express not only a child's feelings and emotions but also his intellectual curiosity.

10

The Art Program

Influence of Early Education

It is with some hesitancy that we put forth our suggestions for a curriculum for art in early childhood. The hesitancy is not because we have no concrete suggestions; we have more than enough of these. In fact, we can draw many conclusions from our work so far. However, our hesitancy is based upon the fact that most programs in early childhood education which have attempted to achieve certain goals have failed. These programs have not failed to achieve an immediate goal, but rather have failed to achieve a long-term goal. Usually children who have been involved in particular intervention programs at the preschool level show gains in scores on a variety of tests. However, these gains begin to disappear as soon as

207

these children start regular school programs; by the time the children have reached the end of the second grade, there is usually no difference between children who have attended a particular program as pre-schoolers and those who have not been so lucky. It should be pointed out that there has been some continued improvement in school achievement if a continuing program augments or supports the disadvantaged child, but without this continued support apparently the effects of an inadequate home or an unsympathetic school environment combine to erase the positive effects of any program at the preschool level.

There are many studies in the literature evaluating a variety of programs in early education. A review of the effectiveness of psycholinguistic training programs for young children compared the results of 38 different training programs (Hammill and Larsen, 1974). Their conclusions were that the effectiveness of these programs has not been conclusively demonstrated. These findings are important when one considers the amount of time, effort, and money that is beng devoted to these training programs in linguistic skills. A report on the longitudinal evaluations of preschool programs prepared for the Department of Health, Education, and Welfare (Ryan, 1974) states that, although preschool intervention programs have an immediate positive impact on children's performances, there are a lot of variables which tend to erode these gains as children grow older. However, there is no doubt that the first years of life are crucial to the development of competency in dealing with life's problems; if children lack the stimulation, support, and environment for learning, they quickly drop below normal in mental development. In discussing the effects of deprivation, Bronfenbrenner (1974) points out that children from disadvantaged families tend to obtain normal scores on tests of mental development before the age of two. But thereafter the level drops rather suddenly and continues to decline as the child grows older and enters school.

The importance of education at the preschool level is not questioned, but the longterm gains of programs aimed at developing particular skills or abilities seem limited. There could be several reasons for this.

One factor that may be worth considering is the usual custom in grade school of keeping youngsters working at tasks that they have not mastered. Once a child has succeeded in solving a problem, reading a sentence, learning how to spell a word, the teacher then sets about finding a task that the child cannot do, and then the youngster must start the procedure all over again. Possibly the advantage that a child had gained from a supportive preschool program does not last very long under these conditions. A second consideration is that other factors such as home life, community, and peer group interaction are important variables which may act together to negate any advantage the child might have had from a good early childhood intervention program.

Creativity and Competency

There is another important consideration. That is, possibly some nursery schools are focusing on the wrong areas. Trying to teach young children factual

107. *Young children manipulate blocks by arranging, balancing, or placing them end to end or on top of one another. This is a natural way of learning relationships.*

material, social behavior, and compliance to teacher's procedures may be artificially imposing a façade upon these children, when actually we should be teaching them how to be nursery school children. From our observations, we have seen that these young children are eager to explore and investigate, are curious about their environment, and spend time building with blocks or painting with no purpose other than enjoyment of the blocks or paint; they react in spontaneous fashion to their environment, are anxious to learn how to spell their names, and will persist in a task of their own choosing. What we advocate is a program that actively involves children and adults in a pleasurable search for competency. This search would reinforce the ways children explore and understand their environment, and the arts would play an important role in that program. We feel it important to encourage curiosity, foster aesthetic sensitivity, develop spontaneous imaginative thinking, and support the learning of skills that will facilitate the interaction of the child with his environment.

Can such a program be more effective than nursery school or preschool programs have been in the past? A study that examined and compared the classroom structure of 13 urban Head Start programs in Philadelphia (Huston-Stein, Friedrich-Cofer, and Susman, 1977) came to the conclusion that the classroom structure is an important influence on children's behavior. Of particular interest is the finding that highly-structured programs facilitated attention to tasks and conformity to adult expectations in group situations. However, they found that this kind of structure is less conducive to the development of self-directing, independent efforts to master motor and cognitive skills or to the generalization of learned skills.

Some of our discussions with teachers indicated that emphasis on certain cognitive skills resulted from their concern that children be prepared to begin a reading program when they reach first grade. One of our studies (Stein, 1972) compared two types of training programs designed to improve the reading ability of 57 kindergarten children. Although there are a lot of programs designed to improve the reading ability of

108. *It is a challenge to master the tool to scrape carrots. For the child, this is an important task.*

young children, the one selected for this study was the Frostig program for the development of visual perception (1964). This was compared with an activity-experience type of program which consisted of some open-ended unstructured experiences: hammering nails into wooden stumps, making popcorn, playing with water, and a lot of drawing and painting. By comparison, the Frostig method involves a lot of work sheets and prescribed activities to ensure that children know different shapes and colors, are able to follow directions, and so forth. There were also control groups, children who merely read books and played games with the teachers; this was to ensure that if any

changes took place it was because of the programs and not because of maturation.

This particular study went on for three days a week, over a five week period. Different teachers taught different kindergartens using the two different methods so there would be no teacher bias. There were a number of pretests, including a reading readiness test, and a number of posttests after the training period was over. The results showed that all children improved in their reading abilities; it did not seem to make any difference which method was used. In fact, the group that improved the most was one small control group who had no activities directly related to reading except for the teacher reading stories that children selected. It was interesting to note that this was also the group that the teacher enjoyed the most, because there was no pressure to achieve, and the children could help decide the activities. There was one additional finding; in all groups those children who were most active in drawing and painting scored higher on reading readiness tests than did those children who did not enjoy art activity.

Numerous other studies done elsewhere support these findings. That is, programs designed by adults to achieve specific objectives which are not understood by the children are doomed to failure. This is sobering when one realizes how much planning goes into such programs. It therefore follows that any program that utilizes the arts, such as the Stein study, must have as its goal not the improvement of a particular skill or certain scores on some test, even an IQ test, but instead must focus upon the development of competency in the young child as a person.

In reviewing our work to date in hopes of finding a direction for a program in the creative arts for children, two things of prime importance emerge. One is that young children are actively involved in extracting information from their environment by tasting, touching, pushing, pulling, listening, comparing, and so forth. It is through such active involvement and exploration that factual knowledge is accumulated. The second important consideration is that information does not in itself constitute learning. This information must be digested or assimilated in such a way that children can deal with it; from what their senses are

109. Children touch, taste, and feel their environment. Opportunities for such first-hand experiences gradually disappear as formal schooling closes in.

bringing in, they must be able to abstract the important and usable and to discard the irrelevant or incomprehensible. We feel that art can contribute tremendously to both of these elements of learning.

Basis for Program Planning

Examining the information that we have gathered on developmental levels of young children's art, we find that there is a steady progression from scribbling to a representation showing a great deal of knowledge and information about the environment by the time the child is in kindergarten. Although occurring at somewhat different ages for each child, the order of these stages does not vary and is interrupted only by artistic asides that we have called aesthetic behavior. To develop a program that is outside or beyond the artistic understanding of children is to make the program meaningless. Therefore, any art activity must be geared to the mental and physical capacities of the child involved. Having a child color in outlines of objects on duplicated sheets, particularly when the child has not handled or touched the objects in question, is ridiculous. Having children dip string into paint and draw it across the paper may be an interesting aesthetic experience for adults who can look at these colors and enjoy how they mix, but for the child this is basically a waste of time. We must also dismiss as irrelevant all of the projects that use a model as a stimulus. Showing a scribbling child a horse to copy would be fairly absurd, but we have observed teachers who tried to influence children to make ashtrays out of clay even though the youngsters just wanted to enjoy the manipulation of the clay and the rolling and pounding experiences. Certainly our experiments with the squares and triangles would indicate that much time is wasted in the nursery school in trying to encourage children to learn tasks which should be left for the child's maturation. The continuous use of different materials in the nursery school is also open to question. It can be concluded from our studies that changing materials has no particular advantage in developing concepts, and it has become evident that the mere introduction of a new or different material will not speed up development.

Having dismissed a good number of the types of activities usually considered art within the nursery school and kindergarten curriculum, it is necessary to make a positive step and to identify those materials and projects that would be within the child's understanding and which would provide the opportunity for the child to express in a two- or three-dimensional fashion the symbols, concepts, thoughts, and emotions that are part of him and are a reflection of his subjective relationship to the environment.

Art Materials

It seems important in any school setting that materials should be readily available to children. These should be on shelves within easy reach; they should be easy for youngsters to use, should require little in the way of cleanup, and should not be limited to a special time of day. Drawing instruments are particularly important to have on hand, such as pencils, thick crayons, felt-tipped pens, and chalk. Of course, paper should be easily accessible; although it is not vital that this be high quality white paper, it is important that the paper not be looked upon as something that no one else wanted, such as the back of printed sheets or discarded wallpaper samples. The drawing that young children do is just as important to them as an adult artist's drawing is to him. Adolescents may question their own abilities and the worth of their products, but this is certainly not true of young children. Their products should be treated with respect, but it is not the picture that the child makes that should be saved and cherished; it is the process of thinking that goes into the picture which is valuable.

A second type of material that should be available is clay. We noted that there seemed to be reluctance on the part of some teachers, particularly in the kindergartens, to have clay readily available. Apparently it was thought to be both expensive and

110. *This is genuine artistic expression. Drawings by children deserve to be treated with the same respect as drawings by professionals.*

111. *Young children are fully capable of handling clay. They can help prepare it for use, then experiment with it in many ways.*

dirty. In the nursery schools many substitutions were made, such as playdough, Plasticene, or thickened starch. Clay is a material that can be dug almost anywhere and is readily available in quantity at any crafts supply house; since the price ranges from an afternoon's work with a shovel to less than the price of substitutes, cost is certainly not an element. Clay can be readily stored in plastic bags, and with the occasional addition of a little water the proper consistency can be easily maintained. Most children are not concerned about having their clay fired. It is easy to toss the products back into the container and to add water to the hardened products so the clay may be reused. Because nursery school children usually do not recognize their own piece of art the following day, and because trying to save hardened clay products is no easy task, it seems a good idea to reconstitute these after a day or two.

112. *When painting large masses of color, the interaction of artist with product is different from experiences either in drawing or working with clay.*

Besides drawing instruments and clay, another important material is paint. In our observations, we found a great variety of paints being used. Often it was an inexpensive powdered tempera paint that took a considerable amount of time to mix and ended up being very runny with lumps of undissolved color. Sometimes soap flakes would be whipped up and mixed with the paint to give it some body, or perhaps starch would be added as an extender. We also found watercolors being used, or food coloring mixed with water and put in small pans, and in one instance even acrylic paint was provided for the children to use. From what we observed, the best solution seemed to be a type of paint that was readily available, did not take the teacher's valuable time to mix up, and was easily washed out of the brushes. Liquid tempera paint seemed to fill all of these requirements. Buying the paint in large quantities reduces its cost and filling plastic syrup dispensers seemed an easy way to be able to distribute the paint and keep it from drying out.

Although drawing and clay work were done at low tables, or occasionally on the floor, painting was apt to be restricted to an easel; this limitation created certain problems. Kindergartens usually had one easel for about 25 children, which meant that only two children could paint at one time, one on each side of the folding easel. Sometimes the nursery school would have more than one easel, but here there were other problems. The most obvious is that paint runs. Every time a small child would pick up a brush full of paint and try to manipulate it, paint would run down the page and drip off the bottom and sometimes even down the handle of the brush onto the hand. A thickener such as soap flakes would slow down this running process, but a child often ended up with a big blob, thus restricting the use of paint to putting down masses of color. The easel was often too high, and children were constantly painting uphill. Probably the easel is merely a holdover from the adult stereotype of what an artist uses. The easel did seem to have value when children were drawing. However, painting done at a low table or on the floor allowed better control of the paint itself.

In one instance we noticed that children enjoyed the use of watercolors; it seems as if the smaller

113. *Watercolors merge and have tonal variations which can frustrate young children, but there are advantages in painting on a flat surface with a small, easily controlled brush.*

brush, the greater choice of color, and the opportunity to control and manipulate the tools were important factors. Painting at the easel with large brushes and premixed paint, with the usual restriction that children painting must wear smocks, seems such a production compared to opening a container of water colors. Because water colors mix easily, too easily for young children who are attempting to put down a definite line, and because the hair brushes splay out in all directions with just a little pressure, it seems more satisfactory to substitute tempera in small containers and small bristle brushes.

Drawing tools, paint, and clay are the essentials for an art program for young children. In addition, scissors should be available, but not plastic ones: it is difficult enough for young children to manipulate scissors, and putting obstacles in their path does not seem to be legitimate. We found some hesitation on the part of nursery school teachers to have sharp scissors available because of the potential danger, but it is difficult for children to cut holes in the center of a piece of paper with blunt-nosed scissors. There might be situations where sharp scissors could be dangerous, but restricting children to poor tools when they are in the process of learning to manipulate them does not seem warranted. Certainly glue — the liquid white glue seems adequate — staplers, and a paper punch or two should round out the list of purchased supplies.

Some nursery schools utilized a good deal of scrap for their art program. This was not found to be true in the kindergartens, where scrap seems to be cleaned up fairly rapidly by the housekeeping staff. On occasion, we saw some interesting collage work being done at all levels. Children would delve into boxes containing pieces of cloth, run their fingers over the cloth, and paste it onto some sort of paper. Sometimes the experience was merely tactile, and the teachers had to encourage the gluing process. Often youngsters would look for a particular piece: a big one, or small one, or dark one, or rough one; it was thought that this was an excellent sensory experience. But we also observed situations in which the scrap material was used in a totally valueless exercise, such as plastic egg containers used to make pretty flowers for Mother's Day, or scraps of cloth cut to prescribed sizes to paste on an outlined form of a person. The teacher may have been creative, but the children usually ignored the prescribed form and enjoyed the texture of the materials. Sometimes interesting colored string, various-sized boxes, colored paper, or pieces of colored cellophane can be utilized. However, we found some children frustrated by a continued use of these materials because they could not control the form or make these materials into symbols.

A few nursery schools had woodworking tools available and soft wood for children to pound nails into or to saw into pieces. It seems strange that the opportunity for this type of work was not available in most kindergartens. Sturdy benches with some sort of vise, small hand tools, and plenty of soft wood are a real attraction. In one instance, some pieces of oak and maple had been donated by a local firm, but these exasperated the children because they could not saw them or drive nails into the hard wood. There is no attempt here to make recommendations for all of the materials which could be used in a school. As used by young children, blocks are an art form. Certainly such things as changing displays, an opportunity to be around live animals, and short field trips all contribute to the interaction a child has with his environment and add a great deal to his art experiences.

Actually it was felt that the materials played a relatively minor role in what the youngster got from the art experience. Probably charcoal on a sidewalk, or wet sand, even a collection of natural materials, or a stretch of smooth mud would all provide a means for youngsters to express themselves. However, we found that most nursery school and kindergarten teachers explained what they were doing in terms of materials. "Last week we worked with cellophane. Today we were lucky to get these nice pipe cleaners. Next week we hope to have some plaster for the children to use." Even some of the books that are designed for those who plan to teach young children seem to treat materials as the art program. One nursery school text put out by the Gesell Institute (Pitcher and Ames, 1975) suggests spatter painting, spray painting, soap sculpture, and even origami folded paper sculpture as being appropriate for preschool children. Our observations indicate that some

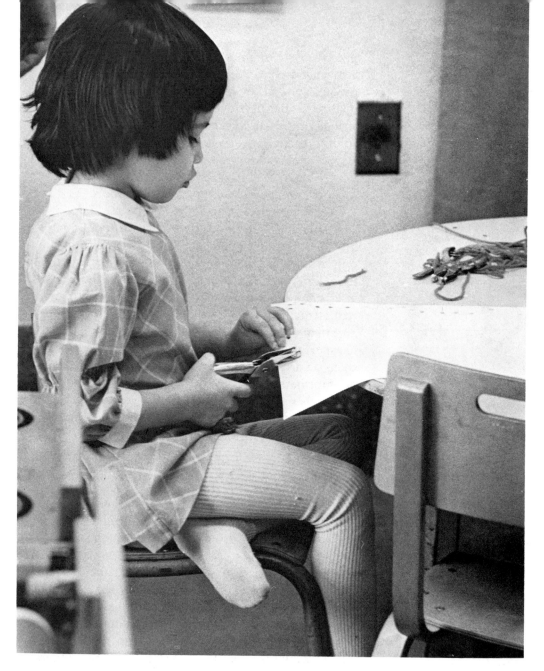

114. *Probably this girl was expected to punch holes to thread the yarn through, but she is content to spend her time punching.*

of these materials would be more appropriate for twelve year olds, but even then it might be wiser to use the soap to wash one's hands rather than to try to make it into sculptured forms.

One additional word might be said about materials. Rarely did we hear nursery school teachers talking baby talk to young children. However, they saw no incongruity in providing these same children with art materials such as playdough, plastic egg cartons, powdered paints, big brushes, large sheets of newsprint, vegetables for printing, all of which are somehow the hallmark of art for young children. These are not the art materials used in the adult art world, but for some reason these are the materials that appeared in every nursery school. Growth is limited with the use of these materials. We wondered why clay, liquid tempera, small brushes, and durable paper were not readily available for these children. We have progressed far enough to realize that using baby talk with small children is not appropriate, but apparently society still believes that it is appropriate to use baby art materials.

Planning Experiences in Art

Young children spend a fair amount of time manipulating art materials, and the art program at the nursery school is an important part of each day. Kindergarteners spend less time in the arts, as preparation for academic subjects expands. By the time a youngster is in the fourth or fifth grade, he may have art only once a week. There is no shortage of verbalization in the literature about the importance of the art experience, particularly for young children. Some authors seem to think that painting, drawing, and working with a whole stack of discarded materials will help develop free, outgoing, sensitive, and perceptive youngsters. Flowery phrases admonish the teacher to give a child the benefit of all that art can offer so that he may develop into an emotionally stable, profoundly feeling and expressive individual, sensitive to human relations, and that through aesthetic expression he may develop a healthy personality. However, from our observations and experiments, we doubt that there is enough evidence to indicate that the arts can automatically perform all of these functions.

Although most of our experiments were aimed at answering specific questions or testing various hypotheses, the children at the Cornell Nursery School were also exposed to short attempts at evolving a different kind of program in the arts. These usually consisted of one particular activity, and sometimes it would be done several different ways. Occasionally we looked at the handling of materials to see if this could be altered to make it less arduous for the teacher to provide art experiences. These brief attempts were evaluated by small groups of interested graduate students, and the resulting comments and suggestions from these sessions comprise a fairly large amount of written material. From these notes some specific suggestions for the art program emerge.

Children need someone to talk to. We had already found that the amount of time a child spends

115. *An adult is a catalyst in the creative process, encouraging curiosity and exploratory behavior.*

drawing increases as he talks to an adult about what he is doing; we also found this to be true in other areas of art. For example, the teacher-type person who merely provides a box of interesting scraps of cloth does not involve the youngster as much as the person who exhibits curiosity about the materials, questions the child as to which one he likes best, wonders if the slippery one or the wooly piece feels better, remarks about how small or big some pieces are, notices differences in color, or asks the child if he saw the ones at the bottom of the box. Although this particular activity was initially thought of as a chance for youngsters to paste materials in an interesting pattern, the pasting part of the session was forgotten in the exchange of comments about the cloth itself. It was only after several pieces were selected that the youngster was asked if he would rather paste these together, staple them on a black piece of paper, or put them alongside one another on a sheet of cardboard. It was interesting to note that most of the five or six youngsters who were involved in this particular session were more inclined to save the pieces they had selected; so for these youngsters no end product emerged. Although this was rather frustrating for the adult, it clearly points out a second factor, that the process is more important than the product.

That the process is more important than the product was demonstrated continually. We have mentioned that children could rarely identify their own pictures the following day, and also that the various steps necessary to achieve a particular end product were often forgotten as children became involved in working, and we also saw many examples of mastery of particular tools without necessarily having a product to show. For example, one session dealt with working in wood, and the children were expected to make a cooperative city with the thought that small blocks would substitute for houses that possibly little bugs or elves could live in. This rather nice romantic idea fell through when it was discovered that the challenge of driving a nail into the soft wood was enough. Dozens of nails were pounded into the wood, and the city for bugs and little elves was forgotten.

Color is not as important as paint. This may sound contradictory because color and paint are

116. *It is more important to have the opportunity to paint than to worry about what colors are available.*

usually considered to be basically the same thing. In one short painting series, children were given fewer and fewer colors to use until, on the last day, they had just blue paint available. It was then noted that the children began to pay more attention to the painting itself rather than spending time mixing the paint or adding one color to another on the paper which invariably ended up being a big gray mass. However, the children were still concerned with the amount of paint or the number of containers they had. If one child had two containers of paint, other children wanted the same number whether the paint was a different color or not. Although only one hand was used for painting, some children asked for two brushes. It seemed as if quantity of paint or quantity of brushes was more important than utilization of these materials for painting. In examining just the blue paintings, it was apparent that there was much less mechanical placing of one brushful of paint on top of another and, as a result, much more painting which developed into some form. Part of this development might be explained by the fact that the earlier sessions had provided the opportunity for experimentation. One painting of a person showed huge hands with large fingers; the child carefully counted the number of fingers as each was painted. Again as with the number of paint containers, it appeared that the number of fingers was important. Whether the fingers were blue, red, or whatever color, did not seem to bother anybody. Even if a wide choice of colors is not readily available, having the opportunity to paint with just a few seems to be a worthwhile experience for children.

Children need to be involved in the procedures of an art activity. Nursery school teachers often put out materials for their charges to play with. Sometimes tables would be ready for children when they came; the clay, drawing tools, or whatever were waiting. As the children finished one activity, they would wander off, leaving behind whatever they had done. It seemed appropriate to us that the children know a little bit about where the materials were stored, help to get them out, enjoy the activity, and help to put the materials away in the cleaning up process. This seemed to work very well for older children, but with younger children our experiment did not work as well. Although these two and three year olds were enthusiastic about rolling out the can that contained the clay, enjoyed seeing the clay in the bottom of a plastic bag, and enjoyed punching the clay and adding water until it was the right consistency, it was at this point that the activity seemed to be over; for the adult involved, this became somewhat annoying. The children had enough experience with the clay just by handling

the material and getting it to the proper consistency, so that the purpose which had been thought through in advance was accomplished, although not in the expected way. This again points out the difference between the adult's concept of an art project and the child's. Some of the observers of our group pointed out that this was an excellent art activity since the children were involved in a sensory experience and had the clear goal in mind of getting the clay prepared; it is sad that an adult should assume that every lesson must culminate in a tangible end product.

Another example of involving children in the whole process took place after they had finished a particularly busy mural which had been done on the floor, with more children painting than had been expected. This mural, as is true of most murals painted in the nursery school, was not a cooperative effort, but it gave the children an opportunity to paint alongside each other. There was no cooperative theme but rather parallel painting. After the mural was removed to dry, the children were encouraged to help in the cleanup process. The adult used the so-called playing dumb method of involving the children by asking the question, "Oh, my, look at the floor, what are we going to do with all this paint?" When several children responded that cleanup was a necessary next step, again came the question, "What shall we use to clean up the paint?" Somehow the solution of wet sponges was hit upon, and the children hurriedly brought back dripping sponges and set to work. The following account is taken directly from the notes of an observer who wrote them from a position of safety behind the screen of an observation booth.

117. *Group painting on the floor can get pretty messy, but the clean-up can stimulate learning and cooperation.*

Dipping a sponge into muddy water and smearing it around the floor increased the distribution of paint and created somewhat of a hazard. Some of this could probably be tolerated. For some children the cleanup process seems more important than the painting activities. With the number of projects going on in the nursery school, one on "cleaning up" might be worthwhile. If children can learn a variety of other things that the staff feels important, knowing how to use the sponge, how to get clean water, and how to put away sponges and mops is just as worthwhile as learning how to blow soap bubbles from Ivory Flakes.

Art must be based upon a child's experience. This sounds somewhat like a truism, but the importance of this fact is often overlooked. One particular youngster seemed to shy away from art activities, especially drawings. Although on occasion he would pick up felt-tipped pens and make a line or two, looking at each color, he was not using these tools for expressive purposes. One of the adults reasoned that, because the child was still in the scribbling stage, we needed to approach him primarily through an enjoyment of the muscular sensations. "Suppose this felt pen were to walk around this piece of paper, just as you walk around the room, how do you suppose it would go?" The idea that the pen could make a mark which was expressive on the page seemed to come somewhat as a surprise to the child. "How do you go around the room? Do you go very slowly and look into each corner or do you go quickly around the room?" These questions created an opportunity for some verbal exchange. "Take this pen and show me how the pen would go around the paper just as if the paper were a room." Although the first strokes were hesitant, the pen was soon hurrying around the paper, and the initial motivation was forgotten as the child became involved in watching the lines and making sounds to accompany the pen strokes.

There were numerous other attempts at putting into practice some of the assumptions which had grown out of an examination of the data that had been gathered. Some of our attempts at working with children in art failed. This raised the question of what made failure and what made success in art experiences. Although difficult to measure, success was seen as the involvement of the child in an activity where he could manipulate, change, or alter the material, and could feel that what he was producing would be uniquely his. The length of time spent in an activity was thought to be one way of measuring involvement, but probably not the only way. Failure was fairly easy to measure because young children are uninhibited about walking off from an activity that does not inter-

118. *As it glides across the paper, a felt tip pen can be expressive and mirror a child's excitement.*

est them. Most of the failures occurred when the plan contained too many steps, was directed toward a specific end product, or was merely mechanical.

As a result of our attempt to make a more workable program in the arts for the nursery school, more questions were raised than were answered. However, there is no doubt that this is an exciting area of learning for children, as our observations and experiments repeatedly reminded us. The curious, eager, creative child is constantly organizing, comparing, and symbolizing his environment through his art. It is a continual learning process and one that we are only beginning to treat with the respect it deserves.

References

Alschuler, R. H., & Hattwick, L. W. *Painting and personality* (2 vols.). Chicago: University of Chicago Press, 1947 (reprinted, 1969).

Bereiter, C., & Engelmann, S. *Teaching disadvantaged children in the preschool.* Englewood Cliffs, N.J.: Prentice-Hall, 1966.

Biehler, R. F. An analysis of free painting procedures as used with preschool children. Unpublished doctoral dissertation, University of Minnesota, 1953.

Brissoni, A. Creative experiences of young children. *Art Education,* 1975, *28*(1), 19–23.

Brittain, W. L. An investigation into the character and expressive qualities of early adolescent art. Unpublished report, Cooperative Research Project (No. 6-8416), Office of Education, U.S. Department of Health, Education, and Welfare, 1968.

Brittain, W. L. Some exploratory studies of the art of preschool children. *Studies in Art Education,* 1969, *10*(3), 14–24.

Brittain, W. L. *Some exploratory studies of the art of pre-school children.* Document No. 70706-WC(8), April, 1970, Office of Education, Contract OEC-3-7-070706-3118, U.S. Dept. of Health, Education, and Welfare.

Brittain, W. L. The effect of background shape on the ability of children to copy geometric forms. *Child Development,* 1976, *47,* 1179–1181.

Bronfenbrenner, U. *A report on longitudinal evaluations of preschool programs* (Vol. 2). Washington, D.C.: Dept. of HEW, Office of Child Development, 1974.

Burkhart, R. C. The relation of intelligence to art ability. In R. Mooney & T. Razik (Eds.), *Explorations in creativity.* New York: Harper & Row, 1967, 246–258.

Caldwell, B. M. *Project Head Start: Daily program II.* Washington, D.C.: U.S. Department of Health, Education, and Welfare, 1967.

Chancellor, J. (Ed.). The palaeolithic age. *Discovering Art,* 1964, *1*(1), 3–16.

Childe, V. G. *A short introduction to archaeology.* New York: Collier Books, 1962.

Clarke, E. C. An investigation into the relation between the developmental stages of scribbling and the developmental stages of the directive function of speech. Unpublished master's thesis, Cornell University, 1974.

Collett, P. H. A study of the relationship between perception and production of a triangle among preschool children. Unpublished master's thesis, Cornell University, 1971.

Corcoran, A. L. Color usage in nursery school painting. *Child Development,* 1954, *25*(2), 107.

Frostig, M. *Pictures and patterns.* Chicago: Follett, 1964.

Gesell, A. *The first five years of life; a guide to the study of the preschool child, from the Yale Clinic of Child Development.* New York: Harper & Row, 1940.

Ginsburg, H. *Children's arithmetic.* New York: D. Van Nostrand, 1977.

Goertz, E. C. Graphomotor development in preschool children. Unpublished master's thesis, Cornell University, 1966.

Golomb, C. *Young children's sculpture and drawing.* Cambridge, Mass.: Harvard University Press, 1974.

Graham, F. K., Berman, P. W., & Ernhart, C. B. Development in preschool children of the ability to copy forms. *Child Development*, 1960, *31*, 339–359.

Hammill, L. C., & Larsen, S. C. The effectiveness of psycholinguistic training. *Exceptional Children*, 1974, *41*, 5–14.

Harlan, C. *Vision and invention*. New Jersey: Prentice-Hall, 1970.

Harris, D. B. *Children's drawings as measures of intellectual maturity*. New York: Harcourt Brace Jovanovich, 1963.

Harter, S. Pleasure derived by children from cognitive challenge and mastery. *Child Development*, 1974, *45*, 661–669.

Heilman, H. An experimental study of the effects of workbooks on the creative drawing of second grade children. Unpublished doctoral dissertation, The Pennsylvania State University, 1954.

Holladay, H. H. An experimental and descriptive study of children's prerepresentational drawings. Unpublished doctoral dissertation, Cornell University, 1966.

Hooper, J. Children's drawings of a table and an adaptation of a Piagetian coordination of perspectives task. Unpublished master's thesis, Cornell University, 1977.

Huston-Stein, A., Friedrich-Cofer, L., & Susman, E. J. The relation of classroom structure to social behavior, imaginative play, and self-regulation of economically disadvantaged children. *Child Development*, 1977, *48*(3), 908–916.

Jameson, K. *Art and the young child*. New York: Viking Press, 1968.

Jones, C. A. Relationships between creative writing and creative drawing of sixth grade children. In W. L. Brittain (Ed.), *Creativity and Art Education*. Washington, D.C.: The National Art Association, 1964.

Kellogg, R. *Analyzing children's art*. Palo Alto, Calif.: National Press Books, 1969.

Kuhn, H. *The rock pictures of Europe*. New York: October House, Inc., 1967.

Lansing, K. M. *Art, artists, and art education*. New York: McGraw-Hill, 1970.

Larsen, S. C., & Hammill, D. D. The relationship of selected visual perceptual abilities to school learning. *Journal of Special Education*, 1975, *9*, 281–291.

Larsen, S. C., Rogers, D., & Sowell, V. The use of selected

perceptual tests in differentiating between normal and learning disabled children. *Journal of Learning Disabilities,* 1976, *9*(2), 32–37.

Lewis, H. P. Spatial representation in drawing as a correlate of development and a basis for picture preference. *The Journal of Genetic Psychology,* 1963, *102,* 95–107.

Liedes, L. A. Disclosures of beauty and ugliness by selected six-year-old children. Unpublished doctoral dissertation, Pennsylvania State University, 1975.

Lippitt, R., & White, R. K. An experimental study of leadership and group life. In Haimowitz & Haimowitz (Eds.), *Human Development,* New York: Thomas Y. Crowell, 1960.

Livingston, H. F. What the reading test doesn't test — reading. *Journal of Reading,* 1972, *15,* 402–410.

Lowenfeld, V., & Brittain, W. L. *Creative and mental growth* (6th ed.). New York: Macmillan, 1975.

Lurcat, L. Etude des facteurs kinesthetiques dans les premiers traces enfantins. *Psychologie Française,* 1962, *7*(4), 301–311.

Marshack, A. Exploring the mind of ice age man. *National Geographic,* 1975, *147*(1), 64–89.

Mauer, E. A study of the immediate effects of selected experiences upon the drawings of preschool children. Unpublished master's thesis, Cornell University, 1971.

McFee, J. K. *Preparation for art* (2nd ed.). Belmont, Calif.: Wadsworth Publishing Co., 1970.

Montessori, M. *The Montessori method* (A. E. George, trans.). New York: Schocken Books, 1964. (Originally published, 1912.)

Olson, D. R. *Cognitive development.* New York: Academic Press, 1970.

Pawlikowski, E. A. Three perceptual tasks for retarded and normal children. Unpublished doctoral thesis, Cornell University, 1978.

Piaget, J. *The language and thought of the child* (M. Gabian, trans.). New York: Meridian, 1955.

Piaget, J. *The mechanisms of perception* (G. N. Seagrim, trans.). New York: Basic Books, 1969.

Piaget, J., & Inhelder, B. *The child's conception of space* (F. J. Langdon & J. L. Lunzer, trans.). New York: Norton, 1967.

Piaget, J., & Inhelder, B. *Mental imagery in the child* (P. A. Chilton, trans.). New York: Basic Books, 1971.

237

REFERENCES

Pitcher, E. G., & Ames, L. B. *The guidance nursery school* (Rev. ed.). New York: Harper & Row, 1975.

Russell, I., & Waugaman, B. A study of the effect of workbook copy experiences on the creative concepts of children. *Research Bulletin,* The Eastern Arts Association, 1952, 3(1).

Ryan, S. *A report on longitudinal evaluations of preschool programs* (Vol. 1). Washington, D.C.: Dept. of HEW, Office of Child Development, 1974.

Sibley, A. G. Drawings of kindergarten children as a measure of reading readiness. Unpublished master's thesis, Cornell University, 1957.

Stein, H. B. A comparison of the effects of two kindergarten training programs on reading readiness and creativity. Unpublished master's thesis, Cornell University, 1972.

Taralon, J. *The Grotto of Lascaux.* Paris: Caisse Nationale des Monuments Historiques, 1962.

Thomas, R. M. Effects of frustration on children's paintings. *Child Development,* 1951, 22(2), 123–132.

Torbrügge, W. *Prehistoric European art.* New York: Harry N. Abrams, 1968.

Trisdorfer, A. A study of the ability of preschool children to copy triangles. Unpublished master's thesis, Cornell University, 1972.

Ucko, P. J., & Rosenfeld, A. *Palaeolithic cave art.* New York: McGraw-Hill, 1967.

Vernon, M. D. The development of perception in children. In I. J. Gordon (Ed.), *Human Development.* Chicago: Scott, Foresman, 1965, 177–184.

Waage, F. O. *Prehistoric art.* Dubuque, Ia.: Wm. C. Brown, 1967.

Williams, S. M. The influence of theoretically derived exercises on copying ability of preschool children. Unpublished master's thesis, Cornell University, 1970.

Index

239